REASON
IN RELIGION

Volume Three of "The Life of Reason"

GEORGE SANTAYANA

ἡ γὰρ νοῦ ἐνέργεια ζωή

DOVER PUBLICATIONS, INC.
NEW YORK

Published in Canada by General Publishing Company,
Ltd., 30 Lesmill Road, Don Mills, Toronto, Ontario.
Published in the United Kingdom by Constable and Com-
pany, Ltd., 10 Orange Street, London WC2H 7EG.

This Dover edition, first published in 1982, is an unabridged republication of volume three of *The Life of
Reason; or the Phases of Human Progress*, originally published by Charles Scribner's Sons in 1905.

Manufactured in the United States of America
Dover Publications, Inc.
180 Varick Street
New York, N.Y. 10014

Library of Congress Cataloging in Publication Data

Santayana, George, 1863-1952.

Reason in religion.
(The life of reason / George Santayana ; v. 3)
Reprint. Originally published: New York : Scribner, 1930,
c1905. (The life of reason / George Santayana ; v. 3)
1. Religion—Philosophy. I. Title. II. Series: Santayana,
George, 1863-1952. Life of reason ; v. 3.
BL51.S4127 1982   200'.1   81-19484
ISBN 0-486-24253-6 (pbk.)   AACR2

CONTENTS

REASON IN RELIGION

CHAPTER I

HOW RELIGION MAY BE AN EMBODIMENT OF REASON

Religion is certainly significant, but not literally true.—
All religion is positive and particular.—It aims at the Life
of Reason, but largely fails to attain it.—Its approach
imaginative.—When its poetic method is denied its value
is jeopardised.—It precedes science rather than hinders
it.—It is merely symbolic and thoroughly human.

CHAPTER II

RATIONAL ELEMENTS IN SUPERSTITION

Felt causes not necessary causes.—Mechanism and
dialectic ulterior principles.—Early selection of categories.
—Tentative rational worlds.—Superstition a rudimentary
philosophy.—A miracle, though unexpected, more intelligible than a regular process.—Superstitions come of
haste to understand.—Inattention suffers them to spread.
—Genius may use them to convey an inarticulate wisdom.

CHAPTER III

MAGIC, SACRIFICE, AND PRAYER

Fear created the gods.—Need also contributed.—The
real evidences of God's existence.—Practice precedes
theory in religion.—Pathetic, tentative nature of religious
practices.—Meanness and envy in the gods, suggesting
sacrifice.—Ritualistic arts.—Thank-offerings.—The sacrifice of a contrite heart.—Prayer is not utilitarian in
essence.—Its supposed efficacy magical.—Theological

CHAPTER IV

MYTHOLOGY

CHAPTER V

THE HEBRAIC TRADITION

CHAPTER VI

THE CHRISTIAN EPIC

CHAPTER VII

PAGAN CUSTOM AND BARBARIAN GENIUS INFUSED INTO CHRISTIANITY

CHAPTER VIII

CONFLICT OF MYTHOLOGY WITH MORAL TRUTH

CHAPTER IX

THE CHRISTIAN COMPROMISE

CHAPTER X

PIETY

CHAPTER XI

SPIRITUALITY AND ITS CORRUPTIONS

CHAPTER XII

CHARITY

CHAPTER XIII

THE BELIEF IN A FUTURE LIFE

CHAPTER XIV

IDEAL IMMORTALITY

CHAPTER XV

CONCLUSION

REASON
IN RELIGION

CHAPTER I

HOW RELIGION MAY BE AN EMBODIMENT OF REASON

Experience has repeatedly confirmed that well-known maxim of Bacon's, that "a little philoso-

Religion certainly significant. phy inclineth man's mind to atheism, but depth in philosophy bringeth men's minds about to religion." In every age the most comprehensive thinkers have found in the religion of their time and country something they could accept, interpreting and illustrating that religion so as to give it depth and universal application. Even the heretics and atheists, if they have had profundity, turn out after a while to be forerunners of some new orthodoxy. What they rebel against is a religion alien to their nature; they are atheists only by accident, and relatively to a convention which inwardly offends them, but they yearn mightily in their own souls after the religious acceptance of a world interpreted in their own fashion. So it appears in the end that their atheism and loud protestation were in fact the hastier part of their thought, since what emboldened them to deny the poor world's faith was that they were too impatient to understand it. Indeed,

3

the enlightenment common to young wits and worm-eaten old satirists, who plume themselves on detecting the scientific ineptitude of religion —something which the blindest half see—is not nearly enlightened enough: it points to notorious facts incompatible with religious tenets literally taken, but it leaves unexplored the habits of thought from which those tenets sprang, their original meaning, and their true function. Such studies would bring the sceptic face to face with the mystery and pathos of mortal existence. They would make him understand why religion is so profoundly moving and in a sense so profoundly just. There must needs be something humane and necessary in an influence that has become the most general sanction of virtue, the chief occasion for art and philosophy, and the source, perhaps, of the best human happiness. If nothing, as Hooker said, is " so malapert as a splenetic religion," a sour irreligion is almost as perverse.

At the same time, when Bacon penned the sage epigram we have quoted he forgot to add that the God to whom depth in philosophy brings back men's minds is far from being the same from whom **But not** a little philosophy estranges them. It **literally true.** would be pitiful indeed if mature reflection bred no better conceptions than those which have drifted down the muddy stream of time, where tradition and passion have jumbled everything together. Traditional conceptions, when they are felicitous, may be adopted by the poet, but they must be purified by the moralist and disintegrated by the philosopher. Each religion, so dear to those whose life it sanctifies, and fulfilling so necessary a function in the society that has adopted it, necessarily contradicts every other religion, and probably contradicts itself. What religion a man shall have is a historical accident, quite as much as what language he shall speak. In the rare circumstances where a choice is possible, he may, with some difficulty, make an exchange; but even then he is only adopting a new convention which may be more agreeable to his personal temper but which is essentially as arbitrary as the old.

The attempt to speak without speaking any particular language is not more hopeless than the attempt to have a religion that shall be no religion in particular. A courier's or a dragoman's speech may indeed be often unusual and drawn from disparate sources, not without some mixture of personal originality; but that private jargon will have a meaning only because of its analogy to one or more conventional languages and its obvious derivation from them. So travellers from one religion to another, people who have lost their spiritual nationality, may often retain a neutral and confused residuum of belief, which they may egregiously regard as the essence of all religion, so little may they remember the graciousness and naturalness of that ancestral accent which a perfect religion should have. Yet a

All religion is positive and particular.

moment's probing of the conceptions surviving in
such minds will show them to be nothing but vestiges of old beliefs, creases which thought, even
if emptied of all dogmatic tenets, has not been
able to smooth away at its first unfolding. Later
generations, if they have any religion at all, will
be found either to revert to ancient authority, or
to attach themselves spontaneously to something
wholly novel and immensely positive, to some faith
promulgated by a fresh genius and passionately
embraced by a converted people. Thus every living and healthy religion has a marked idiosyncrasy.
Its power consists in its special and surprising message and in the bias which that revelation gives
to life. The vistas it opens and the mysteries it
propounds are another world to live in; and another world to live in—whether we expect ever to
pass wholly into it or no—is what we mean by
having a religion.

What relation, then, does this great business of
the soul, which we call religion, bear to the Life

It aims at
the Life of
Reason.

of Reason? That the relation between
the two is close seems clear from several circumstances. The Life of Reason is the seat of all ultimate values. Now the
history of mankind will show us that whenever
spirits at once lofty and intense have seemed to
attain the highest joys, they have envisaged and
attained them in religion. Religion would therefore seem to be a vehicle or a factor in rational
life, since the ends of rational life are attained

by it. Moreover, the Life of Reason is an ideal
to which everything in the world should be sub-
ordinated; it establishes lines of moral cleavage
everywhere and makes right eternally different
from wrong. Religion does the same thing. It
makes absolute moral decisions. It sanctions, uni-
fies, and transforms ethics. Religion thus exercises
a function of the Life of Reason. And a further
function which is common to both is that of eman-
cipating man from his personal limitations. In
different ways religions promise to transfer the
soul to better conditions. A supernaturally fa-
voured kingdom is to be established for posterity
upon earth, or for all the faithful in heaven, or
the soul is to be freed by repeated purgations from
all taint and sorrow, or it is to be lost in the absolute, or it is to become an influence and an object
of adoration in the places it once haunted or wherever the activities it once loved may be carried
on by future generations of its kindred. Now reason in its way lays before us all these possibilities:
it points to common objects, political and intellectual, in which an individual may lose what is
mortal and accidental in himself and immortalise
what is rational and human; it teaches us how
sweet and fortunate death may be to those whose
spirit can still live in their country and in their
ideas; it reveals the radiating effects of action and
the eternal objects of thought.

Yet the difference in tone and language must
strike us, so soon as it is philosophy that speaks.

That change should remind us that even if the function of religion and that of reason coincide, this function is performed in the two cases by very different organs. Religions are many, reason one. Religion consists of conscious ideas, hopes, enthusiasms, and objects of worship; it operates by grace and flourishes by prayer. Reason, on the other hand, is a mere principle or potential order, on which, indeed, we may come to reflect, but which exists in us ideally only, without variation or stress of any kind. We conform or do not conform to it; it does not urge or chide us, nor call for any emotions on our part other than those naturally aroused by the various objects which it unfolds in their true nature and proportion. Religion brings some order into life by weighting it with new materials. Reason adds to the natural materials only the perfect order which it introduces into them. Rationality is nothing but a form, an ideal constitution which experience may more or less embody. Religion is a part of experience itself, a mass of sentiments and ideas. The one is an inviolate principle, the other a changing and struggling force. And yet this struggling and changing force of religion seems to direct man toward something eternal. It seems to make for an ultimate harmony within the soul and for an ultimate harmony between the soul and all the soul depends upon. So that religion, in its intent, is a more conscious and direct pursuit of the Life of Reason than is society, science, or art. For these approach and fill out the ideal life tentatively and piecemeal, hardly regarding the goal or caring for the ultimate justification of their instinctive aims. Religion also has an instinctive and blind side, and bubbles up in all manner of chance practices and intuitions; soon, however, it feels its way toward the heart of things, and, from whatever quarter it may come, veers in the direction of the ultimate.

Nevertheless, we must confess that this religious pursuit of the Life of Reason has been singularly abortive. Those within the pale of **But largely fails to attain it.** each religion may prevail upon themselves to express satisfaction with its results, thanks to a fond partiality in reading the past and generous draughts of hope for the future; but any one regarding the various religions at once and comparing their achievements with what reason requires, must feel how terrible is the disappointment which they have one and all prepared for mankind. Their chief anxiety has been to offer imaginary remedies for mortal ills, some of which are incurable essentially, while others might have been really cured by well-directed effort. The Greek oracles, for instance, pretended to heal our natural ignorance, which has its appropriate though difficult cure, while the Christian vision of heaven pretended to be an antidote to our natural death, the inevitable correlate of birth and of a changing and conditioned existence. By methods of this sort little can be done for the

real betterment of life. To confuse intelligence
and dislocate sentiment by gratuitous fictions is a
short-sighted way of pursuing happiness. Nature
is soon avenged. An unhealthy exaltation and a
one-sided morality have to be followed by regret-
table reactions. When these come, the real rewards
of life may seem vain to a relaxed vitality, and the
very name of virtue may irritate young spirits
untrained in any natural excellence. Thus religion too often debauches the morality it comes to
sanction, and impedes the science it ought to fulfil.

What is the secret of this ineptitude? Why does
religion, so near to rationality in its purpose, fall
so far short of it in its texture and in its results?
Its approach The answer is easy: Religion pursues
imaginative. rationality through the imagination.
When it explains events or assigns causes, it is an
imaginative substitute for science. When it gives
precepts, insinuates ideals, or remoulds aspiration,
it is an imaginative substitute for wisdom—I mean
for the deliberate and impartial pursuit of all good.
The conditions and the aims of life are both represented in religion poetically, but this poetry tends
to arrogate to itself literal truth and moral authority, neither of which it possesses. Hence the depth
and importance of religion become intelligible no
less than its contradictions and practical disasters.
Its object is the same as that of reason, but its
method is to proceed by intuition and by unchecked
poetical conceits. These are repeated and vulgar-
ised in proportion to their original fineness and

significance, till they pass for reports of objective truth and come to constitute a world of faith, superposed upon the world of experience and regarded as materially enveloping it, if not in space at least in time and in existence. The only truth of religion comes from its interpretation of life, from its symbolic rendering of that moral experience which it springs out of and which it seeks to elucidate. Its falsehood comes from the insidious misunderstanding which clings to it, to the effect that these poetic conceptions are not merely representations of experience as it is or should be, but are rather information about experience or reality elsewhere—an experience and reality which, strangely enough, supply just the defects betrayed by reality and experience here.

Thus religion has the same original relation to life that poetry has; only poetry, which never pretends to literal validity, adds a pure value to existence, the value of a liberal imaginative exercise. The poetic value of religion would initially be greater than that of poetry itself, because religion deals with higher and more practical themes, with sides of life which are in greater need of some imaginative touch and ideal interpretation than are those pleasant or pompous things which ordinary **When its** poetry dwells upon. But this initial **poetic method** advantage is neutralised in part by **is denied its** **value is** the abuse to which religion is subject, **jeopardised.** whenever its symbolic rightness is taken for scientific truth. Like poetry, it improves the world only by imagining it improved, but not content with making this addition to the mind's furniture—an addition which might be useful and ennobling—it thinks to confer a more radical benefit by persuading mankind that, in spite of appearances, the world is really such as that rather arbitrary idealisation has painted it. This spurious satisfaction is naturally the prelude to many a disappointment, and the soul has infinite trouble to emerge again from the artificial problems and sentiments into which it is thus plunged. The value of religion becomes equivocal. Religion remains an imaginative achievement, a symbolic representation of moral reality which may have a most important function in vitalising the mind and in transmitting, by way of parables, the lessons of experience. But it becomes at the same time a continuous incidental deception; and this deception, in proportion as it is strenuously denied to be such, can work indefinite harm in the world and in the conscience.

On the whole, however, religion should not be conceived as having taken the place of anything **It precedes** better, but rather as having come to **science rather than** relieve situations which, but for its **hinders it.** presence, would have been infinitely worse. In the thick of active life, or in the monotony of practical slavery, there is more need to stimulate fancy than to control it. Natural instinct is not much disturbed in the human brain by what may happen in that thin superstratum of ideas which commonly overlays it. We must not blame religion for preventing the development of a moral and natural science which at any rate would seldom have appeared; we must rather thank it for the sensibility, the reverence, the speculative insight which it has introduced into the world.

We may therefore proceed to analyse the significance and the function which religion has had at **It is merely symbolic and thoroughly human.** its different stages, and, without disguising or in the least condoning its confusion with literal truth, we may allow ourselves to enter as sympathetically as possible into its various conceptions and emotions. They have made up the inner life of many sages, and of all those who without great genius or learning have lived steadfastly in the spirit. The feeling of reverence should itself be treated with reverence, although not at a sacrifice of truth, with which alone, in the end, reverence is compatible. Nor have we any reason to be intolerant of the partialities and contradictions which religions display. Were we dealing with a science, such contradictions would have to be instantly solved and removed; but when we are concerned with the poetic interpretation of experience, contradiction means only variety, and variety means spontaneity, wealth of resource, and a nearer approach to total adequacy.

If we hope to gain any understanding of these matters we must begin by taking them out of that heated and fanatical atmosphere in which the He-

brew tradition has enveloped them. The Jews had
no philosophy, and when their national traditions
came to be theoretically explicated and justified,
they were made to issue in a puerile scholasticism
and a rabid intolerance. The question of monotheism, for instance, was a terrible question to the
Jews. Idolatry did not consist in worshipping a
god who, not being ideal, might be unworthy of
worship, but rather in recognising other gods than
the one worshipped in Jerusalem. To the Greeks,
on the contrary, whose philosophy was enlightened
and ingenuous, monotheism and polytheism seemed
perfectly innocent and compatible. To say God
or the gods was only to use different expressions
for the same influence, now viewed in its abstract
unity and correlation with all existence, now
viewed in its various manifestations in moral life,
in nature, or in history. So that what in Plato,
Aristotle, and the Stoics meets us at every step—
the combination of monotheism with polytheism—
is no contradiction, but merely an intelligent variation of phrase to indicate various aspects or functions in physical and moral things. When religion
appears to us in this light its contradictions and
controversies lose all their bitterness. Each doctrine will simply represent the moral plane on
which they live who have devised or adopted it.
Religions will thus be better or worse, never true
or false. We shall be able to lend ourselves to
each in turn, and seek to draw from it the secret
of its inspiration.

CHAPTER II

RATIONAL ELEMENTS IN SUPERSTITION

We need not impose upon ourselves the endless and repulsive task of describing all the superstitions that have existed in the world. In his impotence and laziness the natural man unites any notion with any other in a loose causal relation. A single instance of juxtaposition, nay, the mere notion and dream of such a combination, will suffice to arouse fear or to prompt experimental action.

When philosophers have objected to Hume's account of causation that he gave no sufficient basis **Felt causes not necessary causes.** for the *necessary* influence of cause on effect, they have indulged in a highly artificial supposition. They have assumed that people actually regard causes as necessary. They suppose that before we can feel the interdependence of two things in experience we must have an unshakable conviction that their connection is necessary and universal. But causation in such an absolute sense is no category of practical thinking. It appears, if at all, only in dialectic, in ideal applications of given laws to cases artificially simplified, where the terms are so defined that their operation upon one another is

15

involved in the notion of them. So if we say that
an unsupported weight *must* fall to the ground,
we have included in the word " weight " the notion
of a downward strain. The proposition is really
trifling and identical. It merely announces that
things which tend to fall to the ground tend to
fall to the ground, and that heavy things are heavy.
So, when we have called a thing a cause, we have
defined it as that which involves an effect, and if
the effect did not follow, the title of cause would
no longer belong to the antecedent. But the necessity of this sequence is merely verbal. We have
never, in the presence of the antecedent, the assurance that the title of cause will accrue to it. Our
expectation is empirical, and we feel and assert
nothing in respect to the necessity of the expected
sequence.

A cause, in real life, means a justifying circumstance. We are absolutely without insight into the
machinery of causation, notably in the commonest
cases, like that of generation, nutrition, or the
operation of mind on matter. But we are familiar
with the more notable superficial conditions in each
case, and the appearance in part of any usual phenomenon makes us look for the rest of it. We do
not ordinarily expect virgins to bear children nor
prophets to be fed by ravens nor prayers to remove mountains; but we may believe any of these
things at the merest suggestion of fancy or report,
without any warrant from experience, so loose is
the bond and so external the relation between

the terms most constantly associated. A quite unprecedented occurrence will seem natural and intelligible enough if it falls in happily with the current of our thoughts. Interesting and significant events, however, are so rare and so dependent on mechanical conditions irrelevant to their value, that we come at last to wonder at their self-justified appearance apart from that cumbrous natural machinery, and to call them marvels, miracles, and things to gape at. We come to adopt scientific hypotheses, at least in certain provinces of our thought, and we lose our primitive openness and simplicity of mind. Then, with an unjustified haste, we assert that miracles are impossible, i.e., that nothing interesting and fundamentally natural can happen unless all the usual, though adventitious, *mise-en-scène* has been prepared behind the curtain.

Mechanism and dialectic ulterior principles.

The philosopher may eventually discover that such machinery is really needed and that even the actors themselves have a mechanism within them, so that not only their smiles and magnificent gestures, but their heated fancy itself and their conception of their rôles are but outer effects and dramatic illusions produced by the natural stage-carpentry in their brains. Yet such eventual scientific conclusions have nothing to do with the tentative first notions of men when they begin to experiment in the art of living. As the seeds of lower animals have to be innumerable, so that in a chance environment a few may grow to maturity, so the seeds of rational thinking, the first categories of reflection, have to be multitudinous, in order that some lucky principle of synthesis may somewhere come to light and find successful application. Science, which thinks to make belief in miracles impossible, is itself belief in miracles—in the miracles best authenticated by history and by daily life.

When men begin to understand things, when they begin to reflect and to plan, they divide the Early selection world into the hateful and the delight-of categories. ful, the avoidable and the attainable. And in feeling their way toward what attracts them, or in escaping what they fear, they at first follow passively the lead of instinct: they watch themselves live, or rather sink without reserve into their living; their reactions are as little foreseen and as naturally accepted as their surroundings. Their ideas are incidents in their perpetual oscillation between apathy and passion. The stream of animal life leaves behind a little sediment of knowledge, the sand of that auriferous river; a few grains of experience remain to mark the path traversed by the flood. These residual ideas and premonitions, these first categories of thought, are of any and every sort. All the contents of the mind and all the threads of relation that weave its elements together are alike fitted, for all we can then see, to give the clue to the labyrinth in which we find ourselves wandering.

There is *prima facie* no ground for not trying to apply to experience such categories, for instance, as that of personal omnipotence, as if everything were necessarily arranged as we may command or require. On this principle children often seem to conceive a world in which they are astonished not to find themselves living. Or we may try æsthetic categories and allow our reproductive imagination —by which memory is fed—to bring under the unity of apperception only what can fall within it harmoniously, completely, and delightfully. Such an understanding, impervious to anything but the beautiful, might be a fine thing in itself, but would not chronicle the fortunes of that organism to which it was attached. It would yield an experience—doubtless a highly interesting and elaborate experience—but one which could never serve as an index to successful action. It would totally fail to represent its conditions, and consequently would imply nothing about its continued existence. It would be an experience irrelevant to conduct, no part, therefore, of a Life of Reason, but a kind of lovely vapid music or parasitic dream.

Now such dreams are in fact among the first and most absorbing formations in the human mind. If we could penetrate into animal consciousness we should not improbably find that what there accompanies instinctive motions is a wholly irrelevant fancy, whose flaring up and subsidence no doubt coincide with the presence of objects interesting to the organism and causing marked reactions within it; yet this fancy may in no way represent the nature of surrounding objects nor the eventual results, for the animal's consciousness, of its own present experience.

The unlimited number of possible categories, their arbitrariness and spontaneity, may, however,

Tentative rational worlds.

have this inconvenience, that the categories may be irrelevant to one another no less than to the natural life they ought to express. The experience they respectively synthesise may therefore be no single experience. One pictured world may succeed another in the sphere of sensibility, while the body whose sensibility they compose moves in a single and constant physical cosmos. Each little mental universe may be intermittent, or, if any part of it endures while a new group of ideas comes upon the stage, there may arise contradictions, discords, and a sense of lurking absurdity which will tend to disrupt thought logically at the same time that the processes of nutrition and the oncoming of new dreams tend to supplant it mechanically. Such drifting categories have no mutual authority. They replace but do not dominate one another, and the general conditions of life—by conceiving which life itself might be surveyed—remain entirely unrepresented.

What we mean, indeed, by the natural world in which the conditions of consciousness are found and in reference to which mind and its purposes can attain practical efficacy, is simply the world constructed by categories found to yield a constant, sufficient, and consistent object. Having attained this conception, we justly call it the truth and measure the intellectual value of all other constructions by their affinity to that rational vision.

Such a rational vision has not yet been attained by mankind, but it would be absurd to say that because we have not fully nor even proximately attained it, we have not gained any conception whatever of a reliable and intelligible world. The modicum of rationality achieved in the sciences gives us a hint of a perfect rationality which, if unattainable in practice, is not inconceivable in idea. So, in still more inchoate moments of reflection, our ancestors nursed even more isolated, less compatible, less adequate conceptions than those which leave our philosophers still unsatisfied. The categories they employed dominated smaller regions of experience than do the categories of history and natural science; they had far less applicability to the conduct of affairs and to the happy direction of life as a whole. Yet they did yield vision and flashes of insight. They lighted men a step ahead in the dark places of their careers, and gave them at certain junctures a sense of creative power and moral freedom. So that the necessity of abandoning one category in order to use a better need not induce us to deny that the worse category could draw the outlines of a sort of world and furnish men with an approach to wisdom. If our ancestors, by such means, could not dominate life as a whole, neither can we, in spite of all progress. If literal truth or final applicabil-

ity cannot be claimed for their thought, who knows
how many and how profound the revolutions might
be which our own thought would have to suffer if
new fields of perception or new powers of synthesis
were added to our endowmcnt?

We sometimes speak as if superstition or belief
in the miraculous was disbelief in law and was
inspired by a desire to disorganise experience and defeat intelligence. No
supposition could be more erroneous.
Every superstition is a little science, inspired by
the desire to understand, to foresee, or to control
the real world. No doubt its hypothesis is chimerical, arbitrary, and founded on a confusion of efficient causes with ideal results. But the same is
true of many a renowned philosophy. To appeal
to what we call the supernatural is really to rest
in the imaginatively obvious, in what we ought to
call the natural, if natural meant easy to conceive
and originally plausible. Moral and individual
forces are more easily intelligible than mechanical
universal laws. The former domesticate events in
the mind more readily and more completely than
thé latter. A miracle is so far from being a contradiction to the causal principle which the mind
actually applies in its spontaneous observations that
it is primarily a better illustration of that principle
than an event happening in the ordinary course of
nature. For the ground of the miracle is immediately intelligible; we see the mercy or the desire
to vindicate authority, or the intention of some

Superstition a rudimentary philosophy.

other sort that inspired it. A mechanical law, on
the contrary, is only a record of the customary but
reasonless order of things. A merely inexplicable
event, manifesting no significant purpose, would
be no miracle. What surprises us in the miracle
is that, contrary to what is usually the case, we can
see a real and just ground for it. Thus,
if the water of Lourdes, bottled and
sold by chemists, cured all diseases,
there would be no miracle, but only
a new scientific discovery. In such a
case, we should no more know why we were cured
than we now know why we were created. But if
each believer in taking the water thinks the effect
morally conditioned, if he interprets the result,
should it be favourable, as an answer to his faith
and prayers, then the cure becomes miraculous because it becomes intelligible and manifests the obedience of nature to the exigencies of spirit. Were
there no known ground for such a scientific anom-
aly, were it a meaningless irregularity in events,
we should not call it a miracle, but an accident,
and it would have no relation to religion.

A miracle,
though unex-
pected, more
intelligible
than a regu-
lar process.

What establishes superstitions is haste to understand, rash confidence in the moral intelligibility
of things. It turns out in the end, as we have
laboriously discovered, that understanding has to
be circuitous and cannot fulfil its function until
it applies mechanical categories to existence. A
thorough philosophy will become aware that moral
intelligibility can only be an incidental ornament

and partial harmony in the world. For moral significance is relative to particular interests and to natures having a constitutional and definite bias, and having consequently special preferences which it is chimerical to expect the rest of the world to be determined by. The attempt to subsume the natural order under the moral is like attempts to establish a government of the parent by the child— something children are not averse to. But such

Superstitions come of haste to understand. follies are the follies of an intelligent and eager creature, restless in a world it cannot at once master and comprehend. They are the errors of reason, wanderings in the by-paths of philosophy, not due to lack of intelligence or of faith in law, but rather to a premature vivacity in catching at laws, a vivacity misled by inadequate information. The hunger for facile wisdom is the root of all false philosophy. The mind's reactions anticipate in such cases its sufficient nourishment; it has not yet matured under the rays of experience, so that both materials and guidance are lacking for its precocious organising force. Superstitious minds are penetrating and narrow, deep and ignorant. They apply the higher categories before the lower—an inversion which in all spheres produces the worst and most pathetic disorganisation, because the lower functions are then deranged and the higher contaminated. Poetry anticipates science, on which it ought to follow, and imagination rushes in to intercept memory, on which it ought to feed. Hence superstition and the magical function of religion; hence the deceptions men fall into by cogitating on things they are ignorant of and arrogating to themselves powers which they have never learned to exercise.

It is now generally acknowledged that workers of miracles, prophets, soothsayers, and inspired or

Inattention suffers them to spread. divinely appointed men may, like meta- physicians, be quite sincere and fully be- lieve they possess the powers which they pretend to display. In the case of the more intelli- gent, however, this sincerity was seldom complete, but mixed with a certain pitying or scornful ac- commodation to the vulgar mind. Something un- usual might actually have happened, in which case the reference of it to the will that welcomed it (without, of course, being able to command it un- conditionally) might well seem reasonable. Or something normal might have been interpreted fancifully, but to the greater glory of God and edification of the faithful; in which case the inci- dental error might be allowed to pass unchallenged out of respect for the essential truths thus fortified in pious minds. The power of habit and conven- tion, by which the most crying inconsistencies and hypocrisies are soon put to sleep, would facilitate these accommodations and render them soon in- stinctive; while the world at large, entirely hyp- notised by the ceremonious event and its imagina- tive echoes, could never come to close quarters with

the facts at all, but could view them only through
accepted preconceptions. Thus elaborate machinery can arise and long endure for the magical service of man's interests. How deeply rooted such
conventions are, how natural it is that they should
have dominated even civilised society, may best be
understood if we consider the remnants of such
habits in our midst—not among gypsies or professional wonder-workers but among reflecting men.

Some men of action, like Cæsar and Napoleon,
are said to have been superstitious about their own
Genius may destiny. The phenomenon, if true,
use them to would be intelligible. They were mas-
convey an
inarticulate terful men, men who in a remarkable
wisdom. degree possessed in their consciousness
the sign and sanction of what was happening in
the world. This endowment, which made them
dominate their contemporaries, could also reveal
the sources and conditions of their own will. They
might easily come to feel that it was destiny—the
total movement of things—that inspired, crowned,
and ruined them. But as they could feel this only
instinctively, not by a systematic view of all the
forces in play, they would attach their voluminous
sense of fatality to some chance external indication
or to some ephemeral impulse within themselves;
so that what was essentially a profound but inarticulate science might express itself in the guise
of a superstition.

In like manner Socrates' Demon (if not actually
a playful fable by which the sage expressed the

negative stress of conscience, the " thou shalt not " of all awe-inspiring precepts) might be a symbol for latent wisdom. Socrates turned a trick, played upon him by his senses, into a message from heaven. He taught a feeble voice—senseless like all ghostly voices—to sanction precepts dictated by the truly divine element within himself. It was characteristic of his modest piety to look for some external sign to support reason; his philosophy was so human, and man is obviously so small a part of the world, that he could reasonably subordinate reason at certain junctures. Its abdication, however, was half playful, for he could always find excellent grounds for what the demon commanded.

In much the same manner the priests at Delphi, when they were prudent, made of the Pythia's ravings oracles not without elevation of tone and with an obvious political tendency. Occasions for superstition which baser minds would have turned to sheer lunacy or silly fears or necromantic claptrap were seized by these nobler natures for a good purpose. A benevolent man, not inclined to scepticism, can always argue that the gods must have commanded what he himself knows to be right; and he thinks it religion on his part to interpret the oracle accordingly, or even to prompt it. In such ways the most arbitrary superstitions take a moral colour in a moral mind; something which can come about all the more easily since the roots of reason and superstition are intertwined in the mind, and society has always expressed and cultivated them together.

CHAPTER III

MAGIC, SACRIFICE, AND PRAYER

That fear first created the gods is perhaps as true as anything so brief could be on so great **Fear created** a subject. To recognise an external **the gods.** power it is requisite that we should find the inner stream and tendency of life somehow checked or disturbed; if all went well and acceptably, we should attribute divinity only to ourselves. The external is therefore evil rather than good to early apprehension—a sentiment which still survives in respect to matter; for it takes reflection to conceive that external forces form a necessary environment, creating as well as limiting us, and offering us as many opportunities as rebuffs. The first things which a man learns to distinguish and respect are things with a will of their own, things which resist his casual demands; and so the first sentiment with which he confronts reality is a certain animosity, which becomes cruelty toward the weak and fear and fawning before the powerful. Toward men and animals and the docile parts of nature these sentiments soon become defined accurately, representing the exact degree of friendliness or use which

28

we discover in these beings; and it is in practical terms, expressing this relation to our interests, that we define their characters.   Much remains over, however, which we cannot easily define, indomitable, ambiguous regions of nature and consciousness which we know not how to face; yet we cannot ignore them, since it is thence that comes what is most momentous in our fortunes—luck, disease, tempest, death, victory.   Thence come also certain mysterious visitations to the inner mind— dreams, apparitions, warnings.   To perceive these things is not always easy, nor is it easy to interpret them, while the great changes in nature which, perhaps, they forebode may indeed be watched but cannot be met intelligently, much less prevented.   The feeling with which primitive man walks the earth must accordingly be, for the most part, apprehension; and what he meets, beyond the well-conned ways of his tribe and habitat, can be nothing but formidable spirits.

Impotence, however, has a more positive side. If the lightning and thunder, startling us in *Need also* our peace, suddenly reveal unwelcome *contributed.* powers before which we must tremble, hunger, on the contrary, will torment us with floating ideas, intermittent impulses to act, suggesting things which would be wholly delightful if only we could find them, but which it becomes intolerable to remain without.   In this case our fear, if we still choose to call it so, would be lest our cravings should remain unsatisfied, or rather fear has given place to need; we recognise our dependence on external powers not because they threaten but because they forsake us.

Obvious considerations like these furnish the proof of God's existence, not as philosophers have **The real** tried to express it after the fact and in **evidences** **of God's** relation to mythical conceptions of God **existence.** already current, but as mankind originally perceived it, and (where religion is spontaneous) perceives it still. There is such an order in experience that we find our desires doubly dependent on something which, because it disregards our will, we call an external power. Sometimes it overwhelms us with scourges and wonders, so that we must marvel at it and fear; sometimes it removes, or after removing restores, a support necessary to our existence and happiness, so that we must cling to it, hope for it, and love it. Whatever is serious in religion, whatever is bound up with morality and fate, is contained in those plain experiences of dependence and of affinity to that on which we depend. The rest is poetry, or mythical philosophy, in which definitions not warranted in the end by experience are given to that power which experience reveals. To reject such arbitrary definitions is called atheism by those who frame them; but a man who studies for himself the ominous and the friendly aspects of reality and gives them the truest and most adequate expression he can is repeating what the founders of religion did in the beginning. He is their companion and fol-

lower more truly than are the apologists for second-hand conceptions which these apologists themselves have never compared with the facts, and
which they prize chiefly for misrepresenting actual
experience and giving it imaginary extensions.

Religion is not essentially an imposture, though
it might seem so if we consider it as its defend-
ers present it to us rather than as its discoverers and original spokesmen uttered it in the
presence of nature and face to face with unsophisticated men. Religion is an interpretation of experience, honestly made, and made in
view of man's happiness and its empirical conditions. That this interpretation is poetical goes
without saying, since natural and moral science,
even to-day, are inadequate for the task. But the
mythical form into which men cast their wisdom
was not chosen by them because they preferred to
be imaginative; it was not embraced, as its survivals are now defended, out of sentimental attachment to grandiloquent but inaccurate thoughts.
Mythical forms were adopted because none other
were available, nor could the primitive mind discriminate at all between the mythical and the scientific. Whether it is the myth or the wisdom it
expresses that we call religion is a matter of words.
Certain it is that the wisdom is alone what gives
the myth its dignity, and what originally suggested
it. God's majesty lies in his operation, not in his
definition or his image.

Fear and need, then, bring us into the presence

of external powers, conceived mythically, whose

essential character is to be now terrible, now auspicious. The influence is real and directly felt; the gods' function is unmistakable and momentous, while their name and form, the fabulous beings to which that felt influence is imputed, vary with the resources of the worshipper's mind and his poetic habits. The work of expression, the creation of a fabulous environment to derive experience from, is not, however, the first or most pressing operation employing the religious mind. Its first business is rather the work of propitiation; before we stop to contemplate the deity we hasten to appease it, to welcome it, or to get out of its way. Cult precedes fable and helps to frame it, because the feeling of need or fear is a practical feeling, and the ideas it may awaken are only incidental to the reactions it prompts. Worship is therefore earlier and nearer to the roots of religion than dogma is.

At the same time, since those reactions which are directly efficacious go to form arts and industrial

habits, and eventually put before us the world of science and common-sense, religious practice and thought are confined to the sphere in which direct manipulation of things is impossible. Cultus is always distinguishable from industry, even when the worshipper's motives are most sordid and his notions most material; for in religious operations the changes worked or expected can never be traced consecutively. There is a break, often a complete diversity and disproportion, between effort and result. Religion is a form of rational living more empirical, looser, more primitive than art. Man's consciousness in it is more immersed in nature, nearer to a vegetative union with the general life; it bemoans division and celebrates harmony with a more passive and lyrical wonder. The element of action proper to religion is extremely arbitrary, and we are often at a loss to see in what way the acts recommended conduce at all to the result foretold.

As theoretical superstition stops at any cause, so practical superstition seizes on any means. Religion arises under high pressure: in the last extremity, every one appeals to God. But in the last extremity all known methods of action have proved futile; when resources are exhausted and ideas fail, if there is still vitality in the will it sends a supreme appeal to the supernatural. This appeal is necessarily made in the dark: it is the appeal of a conscious impotence, of an avowed perplexity. What a man in such a case may come to do to propitiate the deity, or to produce by magic a result he cannot produce by art, will obviously be some random action. He will be driven back to the place where instinct and reason begin. His movement will be absolutely experimental, altogether spontaneous. He will have no reason for what he does, save that he must do something.

What he will do, however, will not be very original; a die must fall on some one of its six faces, shake it as much as you please. When Don Quixote, seeking to do good absolutely at a venture, let the reins drop on Rocinante's neck, the poor beast very naturally followed the highway; and a man wondering what will please heaven can ultimately light on nothing but what might please himself. It is pathetic to observe how lowly the motives are that religion, even the highest, attributes to the deity, and from what a hard-pressed and bitter existence they have been drawn. To be given the best morsel, to be remembered, to be praised, to be obeyed blindly and punctiliously—

Meanness and envy in the gods, suggesting sacrifice. these have been thought points of honour with the gods, for which they would dispense favours and punishments on the most exorbitant scale. Indeed, the widespread practice of sacrifice, like all mutilations and penances, suggests an even meaner jealousy and malice in the gods; for the disciplinary functions which these things may have were not aimed at in the beginning, and would not have associated them particularly with religion. In setting aside the fat for the gods' pleasure, in sacrificing the first-born, in a thousand other cruel ceremonies, the idea apparently was that an envious onlooker, lurking unseen, might poison the whole, or revenge himself for not having enjoyed it, unless a part—possibly sufficient for his hunger—were surrendered to him volun-

tarily. This onlooker was a veritable demon,
treated as a man treats a robber to whom he
yields his purse that his life may be spared.

To call the gods envious has a certain symbolic
truth, in that earthly fortunes are actually precarious; and such an observation might inspire
detachment from material things and a kind of
philosophy. But what at first inspires sacrifice
is a literal envy imputed to the gods, a spirit of
vengeance and petty ill-will; so that they grudge
a man even the good things which they cannot
enjoy themselves. If the god is a tyrant, the
votary will be a tax-payer surrendering his tithes
to secure immunity from further levies or from
attack by other potentates. God and man will
be natural enemies, living in a sort of politic
peace.

Sacrifices are far from having merely this sinister meaning. Once inaugurated they suggest fur-
Ritualistic ther ideas, and from the beginning they
arts.   had happier associations. The sacrifice
was incidental to a feast, and the plenty it was
to render safe existed already. What was a bribe,
offered in the spirit of barter, to see if the envious
power could not be mollified by something less than
the total ruin of his victims, could easily become a
genial distribution of what custom assigned to each:
so much to the chief, so much to the god, so much
to the husbandman. There is a certain openness, and as it were the form of justice, in giving
each what is conventionally his due, however little

he may really deserve it. In religious observances this sentiment plays an important part, and men find satisfaction in fulfilling in a seemly manner what is prescribed; and since they know little about the ground or meaning of what they do, they feel content and safe if at least they have done it properly. Sacrifices are often performed in this spirit; and when a beautiful order and religious calm have come to dignify the performance, the mind, having meantime very little to occupy it, may embroider on the given theme. It is then that fable, and new religious sentiments suggested by fable, appear prominently on the scene.

In agricultural rites, for instance, sacrifice will naturally be offered to the deity presiding over **Thank-** germination; that is the deity that **offerings.** might, perhaps, withdraw his favour with disastrous results. He commonly proves, however, a kindly and responsive being, and in offering to him a few sheaves of corn, some barley-cakes, or a libation from the vintage, the public is grateful rather than calculating; the sacrifice has become an act of thanksgiving. So in Christian devotion (which often follows primitive impulses and repeats the dialectic of paganism in a more speculative region) the redemption did not remain merely expiatory. It was not merely a debt to be paid off and a certain quantum of suffering to be endured which had induced the Son of God to become man and to take up his cross. It was, so the subtler theologians declared, an act of

affection as much as of pity; and the spell of the
doctrine over the human heart lay in feeling that
God wished to assimilate himself to man, rather
than simply from above to declare him forgiven; so
that the incarnation was in effect a rehabilitation
of man, a redemption in itself, and a forgiveness.
Men like to think that God has sat at their table
and walked among them in disguise. The idea is
flattering; it suggests that the courtesy may some
day be returned, and for those who can look so
deep it expresses pointedly the philosophic truth
of the matter. For are not the gods, too, in eternal
travail after their ideal, and is not man a part of
the world, and his art a portion of the divine wisdom? If the incarnation was a virtual redemption, the truest incarnation was the laborious creation itself.

If sacrifice, in its more amiable aspect, can become thanksgiving and an expression of profitable
The sacrifice dependence, it can suffer an even nobler
of a contrite transformation while retaining all its
heart. austerity. Renunciation is the corner-
stone of wisdom, the condition of all genuine
achievement. The gods, in asking for a sacrifice,
may invite us to give up not a part of our food
or of our liberty but the foolish and inordinate
part of our wills. The sacrifice may be dictated
to us not by a jealous enemy needing to be paci-
fied but by a far-seeing friend, wishing we may
not be deceived. If what we are commanded to
surrender is only what is doing us harm, the god

demanding the sacrifice is our own ideal. He has
no interests in the case other than our own; he
is no part of the environment; he is the goal that
determines for us how we should proceed in order
to realise as far as possible our inmost aspirations.
When religion reaches this phase it has become
thoroughly moral. It has ceased to represent or
misrepresent material conditions, and has learned
to embody spiritual goods.

Sacrifice is a rite, and rites can seldom be made
to embody ideas exclusively moral. Something
dramatic or mystical will cling to the performance,
and, even when the effect of it is to purify, it will
bring about an emotional catharsis rather than a
moral improvement. The mass is a ritual sacrifice,
and the communion is a part of it, having the
closest resemblance to what sacrifices have always
been. Among the devout these ceremonies, and
the lyric emotions they awaken, have a quite visible
influence; but the spell is mystic, the god soon
recedes, and it would be purely fanciful to maintain that any permanent moral effect comes from
such an exercise. The Church has felt as much
and introduced the confession, where a man may
really be asked to consider what sacrifices he
should make for his part, and in what practical
direction he should imagine himself to be drawn
by the vague Dionysiac influences to which the
ritual subjects him.

As sacrifice expresses fear, prayer expresses
need. Common-sense thinks of language as some-

thing meant to be understood by another and to produce changes in his disposition and behaviour, but language has pre-rational uses, of which poetry and prayer are perhaps the chief. A man overcome by passion assumes dramatic attitudes surely not intended to be watched and interpreted; like tears, gestures may touch an observer's heart, but they do not come for that purpose. So the fund of words and phrases latent in the mind flow out under stress of emotion; they flow because they belong to the situation, because they fill out and complete a perception absorbing the mind; they do not flow primarily to be listened to. The instinct to pray is one of the chief avenues to the deity, and the form prayer takes helps immensely to define the power it is addressed to; indeed, it is in the act of praying that men formulate to themselves what God must be, and tell him at great length what they believe and what they expect of him. The initial forms of prayer are not so absurd as the somewhat rationalised forms of it. Unlike sacrifice, prayer seems to be justified by its essence and to be degraded by the transformations it suffers in reflection, when men try to find a place for it in their cosmic economy; for its essence is poetical, expressive, contemplative, and it grows more and more nonsensical the more people insist on making it a prosaic, commercial exchange of views between two interlocutors.

Prayer is not utilitarian in essence.

Prayer is a soliloquy; but being a soliloquy expressing need, and being furthermore, like sacrifice, a desperate expedient which men fly to in their impotence, it looks for an effect: to cry aloud, to make vows, to contrast eloquently the given with the ideal situation, is certainly as likely a way of bringing about a change for the better as it would be to chastise one's self severely, or to destroy what one loves best, or to perform acts altogether trivial and arbitrary. Prayer also is magic, and as such it is expected to do work. The answer looked for, or one which may be accepted instead, very often ensues; and it is then that mythology begins to enter in and seeks to explain by what machinery of divine passions and purposes that answering effect was produced.

Magic is in a certain sense the mother of art, art being the magic that succeeds and can establish itself. For this very reason mere magic **Its supposed** is never appealed to when art has been **efficacy** **magical.** found, and no unsophisticated man prays to have that done for him which he knows how to do for himself. When his art fails, if his necessity still presses, he appeals to magic, and he prays when he no longer can control the event, provided this event is momentous to him. Prayer is not a substitute for work; it is a desperate effort to work further and to be efficient beyond the range of one's powers. It is not the lazy who are most inclined to prayer; those pray most who care most, and who, having worked hard, find it intolerable to be defeated.

No chapter in theology is more unhappy than that in which a material efficacy is assigned to **Theological** prayer. In the first place the facts con- **puzzles.** tradict the notion that curses can bring evil or blessings can cure; and it is not observed that the most orthodox and hard-praying army wins the most battles. The facts, however, are often against theology, which has to rely on dialectical refinements to explain them away; but unfortunately in this instance dialectic is no less hostile than experience. God must know our necessities before we ask and, if he is good, must already have decided what he would do for us. Prayer, like every other act, becomes in a providential world altogether perfunctory and histrionic; we are compelled to go through it, it is set down for us in the play, but it lacks altogether that moral value which we assign to it. When our prayers fail, it must be better than if they had succeeded, so that prayer, with all free preference whatsoever, becomes an absurdity. The trouble is much deeper than that which so many people find in determinism. A physical predetermination, in making all things necessary, leaves all values entire, and my preferences, though they cannot be efficacious unless they express preformed natural forces, are not invalidated ideally. It is still true that the world would have been better to all eternity if my will also could have been fulfilled. A providential optimism, on the contrary, not merely predetermines events but discounts values; and it reduces every mortal aspiration, every pang of conscience; every wish that things should be better than they are, to a blind impertinence, nay, to a sacrilege. Thus, you may not pray that God's kingdom may come, but only—what is not a prayer but a dogma—that it has come already. The mythology that pretends to justify prayer by giving it a material efficacy misunderstands prayer completely and makes it ridiculous, for it turns away from the heart, which prayer expresses pathetically, to a fabulous cosmos where aspirations have been turned into things and have thereby stifled their own voices.

The situation would not be improved if we surrendered that mystical optimism, and maintained

A real efficacy would be mechanical.

that prayer might really attract superhuman forces to our aid by giving them a signal without which they would not have been able to reach us. If experience lent itself to such a theory there would be nothing in it more impossible than in ordinary telepathy; prayer would then be an art like conversation, and the exact personages and interests would be discoverable to which we might appeal. A celestial diplomacy might then be established not very unlike primitive religions. Religion would have reverted to industry and science, to which the grosser spirits that take refuge under it have always wished to assimilate it. But is it really the office of religion to work upon external powers and extract from them certain calculable effects? Is it

an art, like empiric medicine, and merely a dubi-
ous and mystic industry? If so, it exists only by
imperfection; were it better developed it would
coincide with those material and social arts with
which it is identical in essence. Successful religion, like successful magic, would have passed into
the art of exploiting the world.

What successful religion really should pass into
is contemplation, ideality, poetry, in the sense in
True uses   which poetry includes all imaginative
of prayer.   moral life. That this is what religion
looks to is very clear in prayer and in the efficacy
which prayer consistently can have. In rational
prayer the soul may be said to accomplish three
things important to its welfare: it withdraws within itself and defines its good, it accommodates itself
to destiny, and it grows like the ideal which it
conceives.

If prayer springs from need it will naturally
dwell on what would satisfy that necessity; some-
It clarifies   times, indeed, it does nothing else but
the ideal.   articulate and eulogise what is most
wanted and prized. This object will often be particular, and so it should be, since Socrates' prayer
"for the best" would be perfunctory and vapid
indeed in a man whose life had not been spent,
like Socrates', in defining what the best was. Yet
any particular good lies in a field of relations; it
has associates and implications, so that the mind
dwelling on it and invoking its presence will naturally be enticed also into its background, and will

wander there, perhaps to come upon greater goods, or upon evils which the coveted good would make inevitable. An earnest consideration, therefore, of anything desired is apt to enlarge and generalise aspiration till it embraces an ideal life; for from almost any starting-point the limits and contours of mortal happiness are soon descried. Prayer, inspired by a pressing need, already relieves its importunity by merging it in the general need of the spirit and of mankind. It therefore calms the passions in expressing them, like all idealisation, and tends to make the will conformable with reason and justice.

A comprehensive ideal, however, is harder to realise than a particular one: the rain wished for may fall, the death feared may be averted, but the kingdom of heaven does not come. It is in the very essence of prayer to regard a denial as possible. There would be no sense in defining and begging for the better thing if that better thing had at any rate to be. The possibility of defeat is one of the circumstances with which meditation must square the ideal; seeing that my prayer may not be granted, what in that case should I pray for next? Now the order of nature is in many respects well known, and it is clear that all realisable ideals must not transgress certain bounds. The practical ideal, that which under the circumstances it is best to aim at and pray for, will not rebel against destiny. Conformity is an element in all

It reconciles to the inevitable.

religion and submission in all prayer; not because
what must be is best, but because the best that
may be pursued rationally lies within the possible,
and can be hatched only in the general womb of
being. The prayer, " Thy will be done," if it is
to remain a prayer, must not be degraded from
its original meaning, which was that an unfulfilled
ideal should be fulfilled; it expressed aspiration
after the best, not willingness to be satisfied with
anything. Yet the inevitable must be accepted,
and it is easier to change the human will than
the laws of nature. To wean the mind from extravagant desires and teach it to find excellence in
what life affords, when life is made as worthy as
possible, is a part of wisdom and religion. Prayer,
by confronting the ideal with experience and fate,
tends to render that ideal humble, practical, and
efficacious.

A sense for human limitations, however, has its
foil in the ideal of deity, which is nothing but
It fosters   the ideal of man freed from those lim-
spiritual life   itations which a humble and wise man
by conceiving
it in its   accepts for himself, but which a spir-
perfection.   itual man never ceases to feel as limitations. Man, for instance, is mortal, and his whole
animal and social economy is built on that fact,
so that his practical ideal must start on that basis,
and make the best of it; but immortality is essentially better, and the eternal is in many ways constantly present to a noble mind; the gods therefore are immortal, and to speak their language in

prayer is to learn to see all things as they do and as reason must, under the form of eternity. The gods are furthermore no respecters of persons; they are just, for it is man's ideal to be so. Prayer, since it addresses deity, will in the end blush to be selfish and partial; the majesty of the divine mind envisaged and consulted will tend to pass into the human mind.

This use of prayer has not been conspicuous in Christian times, because, instead of assimilating the temporal to the eternal, men have assimilated the eternal to the temporal, being perturbed fanatics in religion rather than poets and idealists. Pagan devotion, on the other hand, was full of this calmer spirit. The gods, being frankly natural, could be truly ideal. They embodied what was fairest in life and loved men who resembled them, so that it was delightful and ennobling to see their images everywhere, and to keep their names and story perpetually in mind. They did not by their influence alienate man from his appropriate happiness, but they perfected it by their presence. Peopling all places, changing their forms as all living things must according to place and circumstance, they showed how all kinds of being, if perfect in their kind, might be perfectly good. They asked for a reverence consistent with reason, and exercised prerogatives that left man free. Their worship was a perpetual lesson in humanity, moderation, and beauty. Something pre-rational and monstrous often peeped out behind their serenity, as it does beneath the human soul, and there was certainly no lack of wildness and mystic horror in their apparitions. The ideal must needs betray those elemental forces on which, after all, it rests; but reason exists to exorcise their madness and win them over to a steady expression of themselves and of the good.

Prayer, in fine, though it accomplishes nothing material, constitutes something spiritual. It will not bring rain, but until rain comes it may cultivate hope and resignation and may prepare the heart for any issue, opening up a vista in which human prosperity will appear in its conditioned existence and conditional value. A candle wasting itself before an image will prevent no misfortune, but it may bear witness to some silent hope or relieve some sorrow by expressing it; it may soften a little the bitter sense of impotence which would consume a mind aware of physical dependence but not of spiritual dominion. Worship, supplication, reliance on the gods, express both these things in an appropriate parable. Physical impotence is expressed by man's appeal for help; moral dominion by belief in God's omnipotence. This belief may afterwards seem to be contradicted by events. It would be so in truth if God's omnipotence stood for a material magical control of events by the values they were to generate. But the believer knows in his heart, in spite of the confused explanations he may give of his feelings, that a ma-

Discipline and contemplation are their own reward.

terial efficacy is not the test of his faith. His faith
will survive any outward disappointment. In fact,
it will grow by that discipline and not become truly
religious until it ceases to be a foolish expectation
of improbable things and rises on stepping-stones
of its material disappointments into a spiritual
peace. What would sacrifice be but a risky invest-
ment if it did not redeem us from the love of
those things which it asks us to surrender? What
would be the miserable fruit of an appeal to God
which, after bringing us face to face with him, left
us still immersed in what we could have enjoyed
without him? The real use and excuse for magic
is this, that by enticing us, in the service of natural
lusts, into a region above natural instrumentalities, it accustoms us to that rarer atmosphere, so
that we may learn to breathe it for its own sake.
By the time we discover the mechanical futility
of religion we may have begun to blush at the
thought of using religion mechanically; for what
should be the end of life if friendship with the
gods is a means only? When thaumaturgy is
discredited, the childish desire to work miracles
may itself have passed away. Before we weary
of the attempt to hide and piece out our mortality,
our concomitant immortality may have dawned
upon us. While we are waiting for the command
to take up our bed and walk we may hear a voice
saying: Thy sins are forgiven thee.

CHAPTER IV

MYTHOLOGY

Primitive thought has the form of poetry and the function of prose. Being thought, it distin-

Status of fable in the mind.

guishes objects from the experience that reveals them and it aspires to know things as they are; but being poetical, it attributes to those objects all the qualities which the experience of them contains, and builds them out imaginatively in all directions, without distinguishing what is constant and efficacious in them. This primitive habit of thought survives in mythology, which is an observation of things encumbered with all they can suggest to a dramatic fancy. It is neither conscious poetry nor valid science, but the common root and raw material of both. Free poetry is a thing which early man is too poor to indulge in; his wide-open eyes are too intently watching this ominous and treacherous world. For pure science he has not enough experience, no adequate power to analyse, remember, and abstract; his soul is too hurried and confused, too thick with phantoms, to follow abstemiously the practical threads through the labyrinth. His view of things is immensely overloaded; what

49

he gives out for description is more than half soliloquy; but his expression of experience is for that very reason adequate and quite sincere. Belief, which we have come to associate with religion, belongs really to science; myths are not believed in, they are conceived and understood. To demand belief for an idea is already to contrast interpretation with knowledge; it is to assert that that idea has scientific truth. Mythology cannot flourish in that dialectical air; it belongs to a deeper and more ingenuous level of thought, when men pored on the world with intense indiscriminate interest, accepting and recording the mind's vegetation no less than that observable in things, and mixing the two developments together in one wayward drama.

A good mythology cannot be produced without much culture and intelligence. Stupidity is not

It requires genius.

poetical. Nor is mythology essentially a half-way house between animal vagueness in the soul and scientific knowledge. It is conceivable that some race, not so dreamful as ours, should never have been tempted to use psychic and passionate categories in reading nature, but from the first should have kept its observations sensuous and pure, elaborating them only on their own plane, mathematically and dialectically. Such a race, however, could hardly have had lyric or dramatic genius, and even in natural science, which requires imagination, they might never have accomplished anything.

The Hebrews, denying themselves a rich mythology, remained without science and plastic art; the Chinese, who seem to have attained legality and domestic arts and a tutored sentiment without passing through such imaginative tempests as have harassed us, remain at the same time without a serious science or philosophy. The Greeks, on the contrary, precisely the people with the richest and most irresponsible myths, first conceived the cosmos scientifically, and first wrote rational history and philosophy. So true it is that vitality in any mental function is favourable to vitality in the whole mind. Illusions incident to mythology are not dangerous in the end, because illusion finds in experience a natural though painful cure. Extravagant error is unstable, unless it be harmless and confined to a limbo remote from all applications; if it touches experience it is stimulating and brief, while the equipoise of dulness may easily render dulness eternal. A developed mythology shows that man has taken a deep and active interest both in the world and in himself, and has tried to link the two, and interpret the one by the other. Myth is therefore a natural prologue to philosophy, since the love of ideas is the root of both. Both are made up of things admirable to consider.

Nor is the illusion involved in fabulous thinking always so complete and opaque as convention would represent it. In taking fable for fact, good sense and practice sel-

It only half deceives.

dom keep pace with dogma. There is always a race
of pedants whose function it is to materialise everything ideal, but the great world, half shrewdly,
half doggedly, manages to escape their contagion.
Language may be entirely permeated with myth,
since the affinities of language have much to do
with men gliding into such thoughts; yet the difference between language itself and what it expresses is not so easily obliterated. In spite of
verbal traditions, people seldom take a myth in
the same sense in which they would take an empirical truth. All the doctrines that have flourished in the world about immortality have hardly
affected men's natural sentiment in the face of
death, a sentiment which those doctrines, if taken
seriously, ought wholly to reverse. Men almost
universally have acknowledged a Providence, but
that fact has had no force to destroy natural aver-
sions and fears in the presence of events; and yet,
if Providence had ever been really trusted, those
preferences would all have lapsed, being seen to
be blind, rebellious, and blasphemous. Prayer,
among sane people, has never superseded practical
efforts to secure the desired end; a proof that the
sphere of expression was never really confused with
that of reality. Indeed, such a confusion, if it had
passed from theory to practice, would have changed
mythology into madness. With rare exceptions
this declension has not occurred and myths have
been taken with a grain of salt which not only
made them digestible, but heightened their savour.

It is always by its applicability to things known, not by its revelation of things unknown and irrelevant, that a myth at its birth appeals to mankind. When it has lost its symbolic value and sunk to the level of merely false information, only an inert and stupid tradition can keep it above water. Parables justify themselves but dogmas call for an apologist. The genial offspring of prophets and poets then has to be kept alive artificially by professional doctors. A thing born of fancy, moulded to express universal experience and its veritable issues, has to be hedged about by misrepresentation, sophistry, and party spirit. The very apologies and unintelligent proofs offered in its defence in a way confess its unreality, since they all strain to paint in more plausible colours what is felt to be in itself extravagant and incredible.

Yet if the myth was originally accepted it could not be for this falsity plainly written on its face; **Its interpretative essence.** it was accepted because it was understood, because it was seen to express reality in an eloquent metaphor. Its function was to show up some phase of experience in its totality and moral issue, as in a map we reduce everything geographically in order to overlook it better in its true relations. Had those symbols for a moment descended to the plane of reality they would have lost their meaning and dignity; they would tell us merely that they themselves existed bodily, which would be false, while about the real configuration of life they would no longer tell us anything. Such an error, if carried through to the end, would nullify all experience and arrest all life. Men would be reacting on expressions and meeting with nothing to express. They would all be like word-eating philosophers or children learning the catechism.

The true function of mythical ideas is to present and interpret events in terms relative to spirit. Things have uses in respect to the will which are direct and obvious, while the inner machinery of these same things is intricate and obscure. We therefore conceive things roughly and superficially by their eventual practical functions and assign to them, in our game, some counterpart of the interest they affect in us. This counterpart, to our thinking, constitutes their inward character and soul. So conceived, soul and character are purely mythical, being arrived at by dramatising events according to our own fancy and interest. Such ideas may be adequate in their way if they cover all the uses we may eventually find in the objects they transcribe for us dramatically. But the most adequate mythology is mythology still; it does not, like science, set things before us in the very terms they will wear when they are gradually revealed to experience. Myth is expression, it is not prophecy. For this reason myth is something on which the mind rests; it is an ideal interpretation in which the phenomena are digested and transmuted into human energy, into imaginative tissue.

Scientific formulas, on the contrary, cry aloud for retranslation into perceptual terms; they are

Contrast with science.

like tight-ropes, on which a man may walk but on which he cannot stand still. These unstable symbols lead, however, to real facts and define their experimental relations; while the mind reposing contentedly in a myth needs to have all observation and experience behind it, for it will not be driven to gather more. The perfect and stable myth would rest on a complete survey and steady focussing of all interests really affecting the one from whose point of view the myth was framed. Then each physical or political unit would be endowed with a character really corresponding to all its influence on the thinker. This symbol would render the diffuse natural existences which it represented in an eloquent figure; and since this figure would not mislead practically it might be called true. But truth, in a myth, means a sterling quality and standard excellence, not a literal or logical truth. It will not, save by a singular accident, represent their proper internal being, as a forthright unselfish intellect would wish to know it. It will translate into the language of a private passion the smiles and frowns which that passion meets with in the world.

There are accordingly two factors in mythology,

Importance of the moral factor.

a moral consciousness and a corresponding poetic conception of things. Both factors are variable, and variations in the first, if more hidden, are no less important

than variations in the second. Had fable started
with a clear perception of human values, it would
have gained immensely in significance, because its
pictures, however wrong the external notions they
built upon, would have shown what, in the world
so conceived, would have been the ideals and prizes
of life. Thus Dante's bad cosmography and worse
history do not detract from the spiritual penetra-
tion of his thought, though they detract from its
direct applicability. Had nature and destiny been
what Dante imagined, his conception of the values
involved would have been perfect, for the moral
philosophy he brought into play was Aristotelian
and rational. So his poem contains a false instance or imaginary rehearsal of true wisdom. It
describes the Life of Reason in a fantastic world.
We need only change man's situation to that in
which he actually finds himself, and let the soul,
fathomed and chastened as Dante left it, ask
questions and draw answers from this steadier
dream.

Myth travels among the people, and in their
hands its poetic factor tends to predominate. It
Its   is easier to carry on the dialectic or
submergence. drama proper to a fable than to confront it again with the facts and give them a fresh
and more genial interpretation. The poet makes
the fable; the sophist carries it on. Therefore his-
torians and theologians discuss chiefly the various
forms which mythical beings have received, and
the internal logical or moral implications of those

hypostases. They would do better to attend instead to the moral factor. However interesting a fable may be in itself, its religious value lies wholly in its revealing some function which nature has in human life. Not the beauty of the god makes him adorable, but his dispensing benefits and graces. Side by side with Apollo (a god having moral functions and consequently inspiring a fervent cult and tending himself to assume a moral character) there may be a Helios or a Phaëthon, poetic figures expressing just as well the sun's physical operation, and no less capable, if the theologian took hold of them, of suggesting psychological problems. The moral factor, however, was not found in these minor deities. Only a verbal and sensuous poetry had been employed in defining them; the needs and hopes of mankind had been ignored. Apollo, on the contrary, in personifying the sun, had embodied also the sun's relations to human welfare. The vitality, the healing, the enlightenment, the lyric joy flowing into man's heart from that highest source of his physical being are all beautifully represented in the god's figure and fable. The religion of Apollo is therefore a true religion, as religions may be true: the mythology which created the god rested on a deep, observant sense for moral values, and drew a vivid, if partial, picture of the ideal, attaching it significantly to its natural ground.

The first function of mythology is to justify magic. The weak hope on which superstition

hangs, the gambler's instinct which divines in
phenomena a magic solicitude for human for-
Myth justifies tunes, can scarcely be articulated with-
magic. out seeking to cover and justify itself
by some fable. A magic function is most readily
conceived and defined by attributing to the object
intentions hostile or favourable to men, together
with human habits of passion and discourse. For
lack of resources and observations, reason is seldom able to discredit magic altogether. Reasonable men are forced, therefore, in order to find
some satisfaction, to make magic as intelligible as
possible by assimilating it to such laws of human
action as may be already mastered and familiar.
Magic is thus reduced to a sort of system, regulated
by principles of its own and naturalised, as it were,
in the commonwealth of science.

Such an avowed and defended magic usually
takes one of two forms. When the miracle is in-
Myths terpreted dramatically, by analogy to
might be human life, we have mythology; when
metaphysical. it is interpreted rationalistically, by
analogy to current logic or natural science, we
have metaphysics or theosophy. The metaphysical
sort of superstition has never taken deep root in
the western world. Pythagorean mysteries and
hypnotisations, although periodically fashionable,
have soon shrivelled in our too salubrious and
biting air. Even such charming exotics as Plato's
myths have not been able to flourish without
changing their nature and passing into ordinary

dramatic mythology—into a magic system in which all the forces, once terms in moral experience, became personal angels and demons. Similarly with the Christian sacraments: these magic rites, had they been established in India among a people theosophically minded, might have furnished cues to high transcendental mysteries. Baptism might have been interpreted as a symbol for the purged and abolished will, and Communion as a symbol for the escape from personality. But European races, though credulous enough, are naturally positivistic, so that, when they were called upon to elucidate their ceremonial mysteries, what they lit upon was no metaphysical symbolism but a material and historical drama. Communion became a sentimental interview between the devout soul and the person of Christ; baptism became the legal execution of a mythical contract once entered into between the first and second persons of the Trinity. Thus, instead of a metaphysical interpretation, the extant magic received its needful justification through myths.

When mythology first appears in western literature it already possesses a highly articulate form. **They appear ready made, like parts of the social fabric.** The gods are distinct personalities, with attributes and histories which it is hard to divine the source of and which suggest no obvious rational interpretation. The historian is therefore in the same position as a child who inherits a great religion.

The gods and their doings are *prima facie* facts in his world like any other facts, objective beings that convention puts him in the presence of and with which he begins by having social relations. He envisages them with respect and obedience, or with careless defiance, long before he thinks of questioning or proving their existence. The attitude he assumes towards them makes them in the first instance factors in his moral world. Much subsequent scepticism and rationalising philosophy will not avail to efface the vestiges of that early communion with familiar gods. It is hard to reduce to objects of science what are essentially factors in moral intercourse. All thoughts on religion remain accordingly coloured with passion, and are felt to be, above all, a test of loyalty and an index to virtue. The more derivative, unfathomable, and opaque is the prevalent idea of the gods, the harder it is for a rational feeling to establish itself in their regard. Sometimes the most complete historical enlightenment will not suffice to dispel the shadow which their moral externality casts over the mind. In vain do we discard their fable and the thin proofs of their existence when, in spite of ourselves, we still live in their presence.

This pathetic phenomenon is characteristic of religious minds that have outgrown their traditional faith without being able to restate the natural grounds and moral values of that somehow precious system in which they no longer believe. The dead

They perplex the conscience.

gods, in such cases, leave ghosts behind them, because the moral forces which the gods once expressed, and which, of course, remain, remain inarticulate; and therefore, in their dumbness, these moral forces persistently suggest their only known but now discredited symbols. To regain moral freedom—without which knowledge cannot be put to its rational use in the government of life—we must rediscover the origin of the gods, reduce them analytically to their natural and moral constituents, and then proceed to rearrange those materials, without any quantitative loss, in forms appropriate to a maturer reflection.

Of the innumerable and rather monotonous mythologies that have flourished in the world, only the Græco-Roman and the Christian need concern us here, since they are by far the best known to us and the best defined in themselves, as well as the only two likely to have any continued influence on the western mind. Both these systems presuppose a long prior development. The gods of Greece and of Israel have a full-blown character when we first meet them in literature. In both cases, however, we are fortunate in being able to trace somewhat further back the history of mythology, and do not depend merely on philosophic analysis to reach the elements which we seek.

In the Vedic hymns there survives the record of a religion remarkably like the Greek in spirit, but less dramatic and articulate in form. The gods of the Vedas are unmistakably natural ele-

Incipient
myth in the
Vedas.
ments. Vulcan is there nothing but fire, Jupiter nothing but the sky. This pa- triarchal people, fresh from the high- lands, had not yet been infected with the manias and diseases of the jungle. It lived simply, ration- ally, piously, loving all natural joys and delighted with all the instruments of a rude but pure civil- isation. It saluted without servility the forces of nature which ministered to its needs. It burst into song in the presence of the magnificent pano- rama spread out before it—day-sky and night-sky, dawn and gloaming, clouds, thunder and rain, rivers, cattle and horses, grain, fruit, fire, and wine. Nor were the social sanctities neglected. Com- memoration was made of the stages of mortal life, of the bonds of love and kinship, of peace, of bat- tle, and of mourning for the dead. By a very in- telligible figure and analogy the winds became shepherds, the clouds flocks, the day a conqueror, the dawn a maid, the night a wise sibyl and mys- terious consort of heaven. These personifications were tentative and vague, and the consequent mythology was a system of rhetoric rather than of theology. The various gods had interchange- able attributes, and, by a voluntary confusion, quite in the manner of later Hindu poetry, each became on occasion any or all of the others.

Here the Indian pantheistic vertigo begins to appear. Many dark superstitions, no doubt, bubbled up in the torrent of that plastic reverie; for this people, clean and natural as on the whole it appears, cannot have been without a long and ignoble ancestry. The Greeks themselves, heirs to kindred general traditions, retained some childish and obscene practices in their worship. But such hobgoblins naturally vanish under a clear and beneficent sun and are scattered by healthy mountain breezes. A cheerful people knows how to take them lightly, play with them, laugh at them, and turn them again into figures of speech. Among the early speakers of Sanskrit, even more than among the Greeks, the national religion seems to have been nothing but a poetic naturalism.

Such a mythology, however, is exceedingly plastic and unstable. If the poet is observant and renews his impressions, his myths will become more and more accurate descriptions of the facts, and his hypotheses about phenomena will tend to be expressed more and more in terms of the phenomena themselves; that is, will tend to become scientific. If, on the contrary and as usually happens, the inner suggestions and fertility of his fables absorb his interest, and he neglects to consult his external perceptions any further, or even forgets that any such perceptions originally inspired the myth, he will tend to become a dramatic poet, guided henceforth in his fictions only by his knowledge and love of human life.

When we transport ourselves in fancy to patriarchal epochs and Arcadian scenes, we can well

feel the inevitable tendency of the mind to myth-
ologise and give its myths a more and more dramatic character. The phenomena of
nature, unintelligible rationally but immensely impressive, must somehow be
described and digested. But while they compel
attention they do not, after a while, enlarge experience. Husbandmen's lore is profound, practical, poetic, superstitious, but it is singularly
stagnant. The cycle of natural changes goes its
perpetual round and the ploughman's mind, caught
in that narrow vortex, plods and plods after the
seasons. Apart from an occasional flood, drought,
or pestilence, nothing breaks his laborious torpor.
The most cursory inspection of field and sky yields
him information enough for his needs. Practical
knowledge with him is all instinct and tradition.
His mythology can for that very reason ride on
nature with a looser rein. If at the same time,
however, his circumstances are auspicious and he
feels practically secure, he will have much leisure
to ripen inwardly and to think. He
will hasten to unfold in meditation
the abstract potentialities of his mind.
His social and ideal passions, his aptitude for art
and fancy, will arouse within him a far keener and
more varied experience than his outer life can
supply. Yet all his fortunes continue to be determined by external circumstances and to have
for their theatre this given and uncontrollable
world. Some conception of nature and the gods

Natural sug-
gestions soon
exhausted.

They will be
carried out
in abstract
fancy.

—that is, in his case, some mythology—must therefore remain before him always and stand in his mind for the real forces controlling experience.

His moral powers and interests have meantime notably developed. His sense for social relations has grown clear and full in proportion as his observation of nature has sunk into dull routine. Consequently, the myths by which reality is represented lose, so to speak, their birthright and first nationality. They pass under the empire of abstract cogitation and spontaneous fancy. They become naturalised in the mind. The poet cuts loose from nature and works out instead whatever hints of human character or romantic story the myth already supplies. Analogies drawn from moral and passionate experience replace the further portraiture of outer facts. Human tastes, habits, and dreams enter the fable, expanding it into some little drama, or some mystic anagram of mortal life. While in the beginning the sacred poet had transcribed nothing but joyous perceptions and familiar industrial or martial actions, he now introduces intrigue, ingenious adventures, and heroic passions.

When we turn from the theology of the Vedas to that of Homer we see this revolution already

They may become moral ideals. accomplished. The new significance of mythology has obscured the old, and what was a symbol for material facts has become a drama, an apologue, and an ideal.

Thus one function of mythology has been nothing less than to carry religion over from superstition into wisdom, from an excuse and apology for magic into an ideal representation of moral goods. In his impotence and sore need a man appeals to magic; this appeal he justifies by imagining a purpose and a god behind the natural agency. But after his accounts with the phenomena are settled by his own labour and patience, he continues to be fascinated by the invisible spirit he has evoked. He cherishes this image; it becomes his companion, his plastic and unaccountable witness and refuge in all the exigencies of life. Dwelling in the mind continually, the deity becomes acclimated there; the worship it receives endows it with whatever powers and ideal faculties are most feared or honoured by its votary. Now the thunder and the pestilence which were once its essence come to be regarded as its disguises and its foils. Faith comes to consist in disregarding what it was once religion to regard, namely, the ways of fortune and the conditions of earthly happiness. Thus the imagination sets up its ideals over against the world that occasioned them, and mythology, instead of cheating men with false and magic aids to action, moralises them by presenting an ideal standard for action and a perfect object for contemplation.

If we consider again, for instance, Apollo's vari-
The sun-god   ous attributes and the endless myths
moralised.   connected with his name, we shall find
him changing his essence and forgetting to be the

material sun in order to become the light of a
cultivated spirit. At first he is the sky's child,
and has the moon for twin sister. His mother is
an impersonation of darkness and mystery. He
travels yearly from the hyperborean regions
toward the south, and daily he traverses the firmament in a chariot. He sleeps in a sea-nymph's
bosom or rises from the dawn's couch. In all this
we see clearly a scarcely figurative description of
the material sun and its motions. A quasi-scien-
tific fancy spins these fables almost inevitably to
fill the vacuum not yet occupied by astronomy.
Such myths are indeed compacted out of wonders,
not indeed to add wonder to them (for the original
and greatest marvel persists always in the sky),
but to entertain us with pleasant consideration of
them and with their assimilation to our own fine
feats. This assimilation is unavoidable in a poet
ignorant of physics, whom human life must supply
with all his vocabulary and similes. Fortunately
in this need of introducing romance into phenomena lies the leaven that is to leaven the lump,
the subtle influence that is to moralise religion.
For presently Apollo becomes a slayer of monsters
(a function no god can perform until he has
ceased to be a monster himself), he becomes the
lovely and valorous champion of humanity, the
giver of prophecy, of music, of lyric song, even
the patron of medicine and gymnastics.

What a humane and rational transformation!
The spirit of Socrates was older than the man and

had long been at work in the Greeks. Interest had
been transferred from nature to art, from the

The leaven
of religion
is moral
idealism.

sources to the fruits of life. We in
these days are accustomed as a matter of course to associate religion with
ideal interests. Our piety, unlike our barbarous
pantheistic theology, has long lost sight of its rudimentary material object, and habituated us to the
worship of human sanctity and human love. We
have need all the more to remember how slowly
and reluctantly religion has suffered spiritualisa-
tion, how imperfectly as yet its superstitious origin has been outgrown. We have need to retrace
with the greatest attention the steps by which a
moral value has been insinuated into what would
otherwise be nothing but a medley of magic rites
and poetic physics. It is this submerged idealism
which alone, in an age that should have finally
learned how to operate in nature and how to conceive her processes, could still win for religion a
philosopher's attention or a legislator's mercy.

CHAPTER V

As the Vedas offer a glimpse into the antecedents of Greek mythology, so Hebrew studies open up vistas into the antecedents of Christian dogma. Christianity in its Patristic form was an adaptation of Hebrew religion to the Græco-Roman world, and later, in the Protestant movement, a readaptation of the same to what we may call the Teutonic spirit. In the first adaptation, Hebrew positivism was wonderfully refined, transformed into a religion of redemption, and endowed with a semi-pagan mythology, a pseudo-Platonic metaphysics, and a quasi-Roman organisation. In the second adaptation, Christianity received a new basis and standard in the spontaneous faith of the individual; and, as the traditions thus undermined in principle gradually dropped away, it was reduced by the German theologians to a romantic and mystical pantheism. Throughout its transformations, however, Christianity remains indebted to the Jews not only for its founder, but for the nucleus of its dogma, cult, and ethical doctrine. If the religion of the Jews, therefore, should disclose its origin, the origin of Christianity would also be manifest.

Phases of Hebraism.

Now the Bible, when critically studied, clearly reveals the source, if not of the earliest religion of Israel, at least of those elements in later Jewish faith which have descended to us and formed the kernel of Christian revelation. The earlier Hebrews, as their own records depict them, had a mythology and cultus extremely like that of other Semitic peoples. It was natural religion—I mean that religion which naturally expresses the imaginative life of a nation according to the conceptions there current about the natural world and to the interest then uppermost in men's hearts. It was a religion without a creed or scripture or founder or clergy. It consisted in local rites, in lunar feasts, in soothsayings and oracles, in legends about divine apparitions commemorated in the spots they had made holy. These spots, as in all the rest of the world, were tombs, wells, great trees, and, above all, the tops of mountains.

A wandering tribe, at once oppressed and aggressive, as Israel evidently was from the begin-
Israel's ning, is conscious of nothing so much
tribal as of its tribal unity. To protect the
monotheism. tribe is accordingly the chief function of its god. Whatever character Jehovah may originally have had, whether a storm-god of Sinai or of Ararat, or a sacred bull, or each of these by affinity and confusion with the other, when the Israelites had once adopted him as their god they could see nothing essential in him but his power to protect them in the lands they had conquered.

To this exclusive devotion of Jehovah to Israel, Israel responded by a devotion to Jehovah no less exclusive. They neglected, when at home, the worship of every other divinity, and later even while travelling abroad; and they tended to deny altogether, first the comparable power and finally even the existence of other gods.

Israel was a small people overshadowed by great empires, and its political situation was always **Problems** highly precarious. After a brief period **involved.** of comparative vigour under David and Solomon (a period afterward idealised with that oriental imagination which, creating so few glories, dreams of so many) they declined visibly toward an inevitable absorption by their neighbours. But, according to the significance which religion then had in Israel, the ruin of the state would have put Jehovah's honour and power in jeopardy. The nation and its god were like body and soul; it occurred to no one as yet to imagine that the one could survive the other. A few sceptical and unpatriotic minds, despairing of the republic, might turn to the worship of Baal or of the stars invoked by the Assyrians, hoping thus to save themselves and their private fortunes by a timely change of allegiance. But the true Jew had a vehement and unshakable spirit. He could not allow the waywardness of events to upset his convictions or the cherished habits of his soul. Accordingly he bethought himself of a new way of explaining and meeting the imminent catastrophe.

The prophets, for to them the revolution in question was due, conceived that the cause of Israel's misfortunes might be not Jehovah's weakness but his wrath—a wrath kindled against the immorality, lukewarmness, and infidelity of the people. Repentance and a change of life, together with a purification of the cultus, would bring back prosperity. It was too late, perhaps, to rescue the whole state. But a remnant might be saved like a brand from the burning, to be the nucleus of a great restoration, the seed of a mighty people that should live for ever in godliness and plenty. Jehovah's power would thus be vindicated, even if Israel were ruined; nay, his power would be magnified beyond anything formerly conceived, since now the great powers of Asia would be represented as his instruments in the chastisement of his people.

These views, if we regarded them from the standpoint common in theology as attempts to re-express the primitive faith, would have to be condemned as absolutely heretical and spurious. But the prophets were not interpreting documents or traditions; they were publishing their own political experience. They were themselves inspired. They saw the identity of virtue and happiness, the dependence of success upon conduct. This new truth they announced in traditional language by saying that Jehovah's favour was to be won only by righteousness and that vice and folly alienated his good-

The prophets put new wine in old bottles.

will. Their moral insight was genuine; yet by
virtue of the mythical expression they could not
well avoid and in respect to the old orthodoxy,
their doctrine was a subterfuge, the first of those
after-thoughts and ingenious reinterpretations by
which faith is continually forced to cover up its
initial blunders. For the Jews had believed that
with such a God they were safe in any case; but
now they were told that, to retain his protection,
they must practice just those virtues by which the
heathen also might have been made prosperous and
great. It was a true doctrine, and highly salu-
tary, but we need not wonder that before being
venerated the prophets were stoned.

The ideal of this new prophetic religion was still
wholly material and political. The virtues, emphasised and made the chief mark of a religious life,
were recommended merely as magic means to propitiate the deity, and consequently to insure public prosperity. The thought that virtue is a natural excellence, the ideal expression of human life,
could not be expected to impress those vehement
barbarians any more than it has impressed their
myriad descendants and disciples, Jewish, Christian, or Moslem. Yet superstitious as the new
faith still remained, and magical as was the efficacy
it attributed to virtue, the fact that virtue rather
than burnt offerings was now endowed with miraculous influence and declared to win the favour
of heaven, proved two things most creditable to
the prophets: in the first place, they themselves

loved virtue, else they would hardly have imagined
that Jehovah loved it, or have believed it to be
the only path to happiness; and in the second place,
they saw that public events depend on men's character and conduct, not on omens, sacrifices, or intercessions. There was accordingly a sense for
both moral and political philosophy in these inspired orators. By assigning a magic value to
morality they gave a moral value to religion. The
immediate aim of this morality—to propitiate Jehovah—was indeed imaginary, and its ultimate aim
—to restore the kingdom of Israel—was worldly;
yet that imaginary aim covered, in the form of a
myth, a sincere consecration to the ideal, while the
worldly purpose led to an almost scientific conception of the principles and movement of earthly
things.

To this transformation in the spirit of the law,
another almost as important corresponded in the
Inspiration letter. Scripture was codified, pro-
and claimed, and given out formally to be
authority. inspired by Jehovah and written by
Moses. That all traditions, legends, and rites were
inspired and sacred was a matter of course in antiquity. Nature was full of gods, and the mind,
with its unaccountable dreams and powers, could
not be without them. Its inventions could not
be less oracular than the thunder or the flight of
birds. Israel, like every other nation, thought its
traditions divine. These traditions, however, had
always been living and elastic; the prophets them-

selves gave proof that inspiration was still a vital
and human thing. It is all the more remarkable,
therefore, that while the prophets were preparing
their campaign, under pressure of the same threatened annihilation, the same puritanical party
should have edited a new code of laws and attributed it retroactively to Moses. While the
prophet's lips were being touched by the coal of
fire, the priests and king in their conclave were
establishing the Bible and the Church. It is easy
to suspect, from the accounts we have, that a pious
fraud was perpetrated on this occasion; but perhaps the finding of a forgotten book of the Law and
its proclamation by Josiah, after consulting a certain prophetess, were not so remote in essence from
prophetic sincerity. In an age when every prophet, seeing what was needful politically, could cry,
" So saith the Lord," it could hardly be illegitimate for the priests, seeing what was expedient
legally, to declare, " So said Moses." Conscience,
in a primitive and impetuous people, may express
itself in an apocryphal manner which in a critical
age conscience would altogether exclude. It would
have been hardly conceivable that what was obviously right and necessary should not be the will
of Jehovah, manifested of old to the fathers in
the desert and now again whispered in their children's hearts. To contrive a stricter observance
was an act at once of experimental prudence—a
means of making destiny, perhaps, less unfavour-
able—and an act of more fervent worship—a re-

newal of faith in Jehovah, to whose hands the
nation was intrusted more solemnly and irrevoca-
bly than ever.

This pious experiment failed most signally. Jerusalem was taken, the Temple destroyed, and the
Beginnings flower of the people carried into exile.
of the The effect of failure, however, was not
Church. to discredit the Law and the Covenant,
now once for all adopted by the unshakable Jews.
On the contrary, when they returned from exile
they re-established the theocracy with greater
rigour than ever, adding all the minute observances, ritualistic and social, enshrined in Leviticus.
Israel became an ecclesiastical community. The
Temple, half fortress, half sanctuary, resounded
with perpetual psalms. Piety was fed on a sense
at once of consecration and of guidance. All was
prescribed, and to fulfil the Law, precisely because
it involved so complete and, as the world might
say, so arbitrary a regimen, became a precious sacrifice, a continual act of religion.

Dogmas are at their best when nobody denies
them, for then their falsehood sleeps, like that of
an unconscious metaphor, and their moral function is discharged instinctively. They count and
are not defined, and the side of them that is not
Bigotry deceptive is the one that comes for-
turned into a ward. What was condemnable in the
principle. Jews was not that they asserted the divinity of their law, for that they did with substantial sincerity and truth. Their crime is to have

denied the equal prerogative of other nations' laws and deities, for this they did, not from critical insight or intellectual scruples, but out of pure bigotry, conceit, and stupidity. They did not want other nations also to have a god. The moral government of the world, which the Jews are praised for having first asserted, did not mean for them that nature shows a generic benevolence toward life and reason wherever these arise. Such a moral government might have been conceived by a pagan philosopher and was not taught in Israel until, selfishness having been outgrown, the birds and the heathen were also placed under divine protection. What the moral government of things meant when it was first asserted was that Jehovah expressly directed the destinies of heathen nations and the course of nature itself for the final glorification of the Jews.

No civilised people had ever had such pretensions before. They all recognised one another's religions, if not as literally true (for some familiarity is needed to foster that illusion), certainly as more or less sacred and significant. Had the Jews not rendered themselves odious to mankind by this arrogance, and taught Christians and Moslems the same fanaticism, the nature of religion would not have been falsified among us and we should not now have so much to apologise for and to retract.

Israel's calamities, of which the prophets saw only the beginning, worked a notable spiritualisa-

tion in its religion. The happy thought of attributing misfortune to wickedness remained a perma-

Penance accepted. nent element in the creed; but as no
scrupulous administration of rites, no
puritanism, no good conscience, could avail to improve the political situation, it became needful for
the faithful to reconsider their idea of happiness.
Since holiness must win divine favour, and Israel
was undoubtedly holy, the marks of divine favour
must be looked for in Israel's history. To have been
brought in legendary antiquity out of Egypt was
something; to have been delivered from captivity
in Babylon was more; yet these signs of favour
could not suffice unless they were at the same time
emblems of hope. But Jewish life had meantime
passed into a new phase: it had become pietistic,
priestly, almost ascetic. Such is the might of suffering, that a race whose nature and traditions were
alike positivistic could for the time being find it
sweet to wash its hands among the innocent, to
love the beauty of the Lord's house, and to praise
him for ever and ever. It was agreed and settled
beyond cavil that God loved his people and continually blessed them, and yet in the world of men
tribulation after tribulation did not cease to fall
upon them. There was no issue but to assert (what
so chastened a spirit could now understand) that
tribulation endured for the Lord was itself blessed-
ness, and the sign of some mystical election.
Whom the Lord loveth he chasteneth; so the
chosen children of God were, without paradox, to

be looked for among the most unfortunate of earth's children.

The prophets and psalmists had already shown some beginnings of this asceticism or inverted **Christianity combines optimism and asceticism.** worldliness. The Essenes and the early Christians made an explicit reversal of ancient Jewish conceptions on this point the corner-stone of their morality. True, the old positivism remained in the background. Tribulation was to be short-lived. Very soon the kingdom of God would be established and a dramatic exchange of places would ensue between the proud and the humble. The mighty would be hurled from their seat, the lowly filled with good things. Yet insensibly the conception of a kingdom of God, of a theocracy, receded or became spiritualised. The joys of it were finally conceived as immaterial altogether, contemplative, and reserved for a life after death. Although the official and literal creed still spoke of a day of judgment, a resurrection of the body, and a New Jerusalem, these things were instinctively taken by Christian piety in a more or less symbolic sense. A longing for gross spectacular greatness, prolonged life, and many children, after the good old Hebraic fashion, had really nothing to do with the Christian notion of salvation. Salvation consisted rather in having surrendered all desire for such things, and all expectation of happiness to be derived from them. Thus the prophet's doctrine that not prosperity absolutely and unconditionally, but prosperity merited by virtue, was the portion of God's people changed by insensible gradations to an ascetic belief that prosperity was altogether alien to virtue and that a believer's true happiness would be such as Saint Francis paints it: upon some blustering winter's night, after a long journey, to have the convent door shut in one's face with many muttered threats and curses.

In the history of Jewish and Christian ethics the pendulum has swung between irrational extremes, without ever stopping at that point of equilibrium at which alone rest is possible. Yet this point was sometimes traversed and included in the gyrations of our tormented ancestral conscience. It was passed, for example, at the moment when the prophets saw that it was human interest that governed right and wrong and conduct that created destiny. But the mythical form in which this novel principle naturally presented itself to the prophets' minds, and the mixture of superstition and national bigotry which remained in their philosophy, contaminated its truth and were more prolific and contagious than its rational elements. Hence the incapacity of so much subsequent thinking to reach clear ideas, and the failure of Christianity, with its prolonged discipline and opportunities, to establish a serious moral education. The perpetual painful readjustments of the last twenty centuries have been adjustments to false facts and imaginary laws; so that neither could a worthy conception of pros-

Reason smothered between the two.

perity and of the good be substituted for heathen and Hebrew crudities on that subject, nor could the natural goals of human endeavour come to be recognised and formulated, but all was left to blind impulse or chance tradition.

These defeats of reason are not to be wondered at, if we may indeed speak of the defeat of what never has led an army. The primitive naturalism of the Hebrews was not yet superseded by prophetic doctrines when a new form of materialism arose to stifle and denaturalise what was rational in those doctrines. Even before hope of earthly empire to be secured by Jehovah's favour had quite vanished, claims had arisen to supernatural knowledge founded on revelation. Mythology took a wholly new shape and alliance with God acquired a new meaning and implication. For mythology grew, so to speak, double; moral or naturalistic myths were now reinforced by others of a historical character, to the effect that the former myths had been revealed supernaturally. At the same time the sign of divine protection and favour ceased to be primarily political. Religion now chiefly boasted to possess the Truth, and with the Truth to possess the secret of a perfectly metaphysical and posthumous happiness. Revelation, enigmatically contained in Scripture, found its necessary explication in theology, while the priests, now guardians of the keys of heaven, naturally enlarged their authority over the earth. In fine, the poetic legends and patri-

Religion made an institution.

archal worship that had formerly made up the religion of Israel were transformed into two concrete and formidable engines—the Bible and the Church.

CHAPTER VI

THE CHRISTIAN EPIC

Revolutions are ambiguous things. Their success is generally proportionate to their power of
The essence of the good not adventitious but expressive.
adaptation and to the reabsorption within them of what they rebelled against. A thousand reforms have left the world as corrupt as ever, for each successful reform has founded a new institution, and this institution has bred its new and congenial abuses. What is capable of truly purifying the world is not the mere agitation of its elements, but their organisation into a natural body that shall exude what redounds and absorb or generate what is lacking to the perfect expression of its soul.

Whence fetch this seminal force and creative ideal? It must evidently lie already in the matter it is to organise; otherwise it would have no affinity to that matter, no power over it, and no ideality or value in respect to the existences whose standard and goal it was to be. There can be no goods antecedent to the natures they benefit, no ideals prior to the wills they define. A revolution must find its strength and legitimacy not in the reformer's conscience and dream but in the temper of that society which he would transform; for no transformation is either permanent or desirable which does not forward the spontaneous life of the world, advancing those issues toward which it is already inwardly directed. How should a gospel bring glad tidings, save by announcing what was from the beginning native to the heart?

No judgment could well be shallower, therefore, than that which condemns a great religion for not

A universal religion must interpret the whole world.

being faithful to that local and partial impulse which may first have launched it into the world. A great religion has something better to consider: the conscience and imagination of those it ministers to. The prophet who announced it first was a prophet only because he had a keener sense and clearer premonition than other men of their common necessities; and he loses his function and is a prophet no longer when the public need begins to outrun his intuitions. Could Hebraism spread over the Roman Empire and take the name of Christianity without adding anything to its native inspiration? Is it to be lamented that we are not all Jews? Yet what makes the difference is not the teaching of Jesus —which is pure Hebraism reduced to its spiritual essence—but the worship of Christ—something perfectly Greek. Christianity would have remained a Jewish sect had it not been made at once speculative, universal, and ideal by the infusion of Greek thought, and at the same time plastic and devotional by the adoption of pagan habits. The incarnation of God in man, and the divinisation of man in God are pagan conceptions, expressions of pagan religious sentiment and philosophy. Yet what would Christianity be without them? It would have lost not only its theology, which might be spared, but its spiritual aspiration, its artistic affinities, and the secret of its metaphysical charity and joy. It would have remained unconscious, as the Gospel is, that the hand or the mind of man can ever construct anything. Among the Jews there were no liberal interests for the ideal to express. They had only elementary human experience—the perpetual Oriental round of piety and servitude in the bosom of a scorched, exhausted country. A disillusioned eye, surveying such a world, could find nothing there to detain it; religion, when wholly spiritual, could do nothing but succour the afflicted, understand and forgive the sinful, and pass through the sad pageant of life unspotted and resigned. Its pity for human ills would go hand in hand with a mystic plebeian insensibility to natural excellence. It would breathe what Tacitus, thinking of the liberal life, could call *odium generis humani;* it would be inimical to human genius.

There were, we may say, two things in Apostolic **Double** teaching which rendered it capable of **appeal of** converting the world. One was the **Christianity.** later Jewish morality and mysticism, beautifully expressed in Christ's parables and maxims, and illustrated by his miracles, those cures and absolutions which he was ready to dispense, whatever their sins, to such as called upon his name. This democratic and untrammelled charity could powerfully appeal to an age disenchanted with the world, and especially to those lower classes which pagan polity had covered with scorn and condemned to hopeless misery. The other point of contact which early Christianity had with the public need was the theme it offered to contemplation, the philosophy of history which it introduced into the western world, and the delicious unfathomable mysteries into which it launched the fancy. Here, too, the figure of Christ was the centre for all eyes. Its lowliness, its simplicity, its humanity were indeed, for a while, obstacles to its acceptance; they did not really lend themselves to the metaphysical interpretation which was required. Yet even Greek fable was not without its Apollo tending flocks and its Demeter mourning for her lost child and serving in meek disguise the child of another. Feeling was ripe for a mythology loaded with pathos. The humble life, the homilies, the sufferings of Jesus could be felt in all their incomparable beauty all the more when the tenderness and tragedy of them, otherwise too poignant, were relieved by the story of his miraculous birth, his glorious resurrection, and his restored divinity.

The gospel, thus grown acceptable to the pagan mind, was, however, but a grain of mustard-seed

destined to branch and flower in its new soil in
a miraculous manner. Not only was the Greek and
Roman to refresh himself under its shade, but birds
of other climates were to build their nests, at least
for a season, in its branches. Hebraism, when
thus expanded and paganised, showed many new
characteristics native to the minds which had now
adopted and transformed it. The Jews, for in-
Hebrew stance, like other Orientals, had a fig-
metaphors urative way of speaking and thinking;
become
Greek myths. their poetry and religion were full of
the most violent metaphors. Now to the classic
mind violent and improper metaphors were abhor-
rent. Uniting, as it did, clear reason with lively
fancy, it could not conceive one thing to *be* another, nor relish the figure of speech that so described it, hoping by that unthinkable phrase to
suggest its affinities. But the classic mind could
well conceive transformation, of which indeed nature is full; and in Greek fables anything might
change its form, become something else, and display its plasticity, not by imperfectly being many
things at once, but by being the perfection of many
things in succession. While metaphor was thus
unintelligible and confusing to the Greek, metamorphosis was perfectly familiar to him. Wherever Hebrew tradition, accordingly, used violent
metaphors, puzzling to the Greek Christian, he
rationalised them by imagining a metamorphosis
instead; thus, for instance, the metaphors of the
Last Supper, so harmless and vaguely satisfying

to an Oriental audience, became the doctrine of transubstantiation—a doctrine where images are indeed lacking to illustrate the concepts, but where the concepts themselves are not confused. For that bread should *become* flesh and wine blood is not impossible, seeing that the change occurs daily in digestion; what the assertion in this case contradicts is merely the evidence of sense.

Thus at many a turn in Christian tradition a metaphysical mystery takes the place of a poetic figure; the former now expressing by a little miraculous drama the emotion which the latter expressed by a tentative phrase. And the emotion is thereby immensely clarified and strengthened; it is, in fact, for the first time really expressed. For the idea that Christ stands upon the altar and mingles still with our human flesh is an explicit assertion that his influence and love are perpetual; whereas the original parable revealed at most the wish and aspiration, contrary to fact, that they might have been so. By substituting embodiment for allegory, the Greek mind thus achieved something very congenial to its habits: it imagined the full and adequate expression, not in words but in existences, of the emotion to be conveyed. The Eucharist is to the Last Supper what a centaur is to a horseman or a tragedy to a song. Similarly a Dantesque conception of hell and paradise embodies in living detail the innocent apologue in the gospel about a separation of the sheep from the goats. The result is a chimerical metaphysics, containing much which, in reference to existing facts, is absurd; but that metaphysics, when taken for what it truly is, a new mythology, utters the subtler secrets of the new religion not less ingeniously and poetically than pagan mythology reflected the daily shifts in nature and in human life.

Metaphysics became not only a substitute for allegory but at the same time a background for

Hebrew philosophy of history identified with Platonic cosmology.

history. Neo-Platonism had enlarged, in a way suited to the speculative demands of the time, the cosmos conceived by Greek science. In an intelligible region, unknown to cosmography and peopled at first by the Platonic ideas and afterward by Aristotle's solitary God, there was now the Absolute One, too exalted for any predicates, but manifesting its essence in the first place in a supreme Intelligence, the second hypostasis of a Trinity; and in the second place in the Soul of the World, the third hypostasis, already relative to natural existence. Now the Platonists conceived these entities to be permanent and immutable; the physical world itself had a meaning and an expressive value, like a statue, but no significant history. When the Jewish notion of creation and divine government of the world presented itself to the Greeks, they hastened to assimilate it to their familiar notions of imitation, expression, finality, and significance. And when the Christians spoke of Christ as the Son of God, who now

sat at his right hand in the heavens, their **Pla-**
tonic disciples immediately thought of the Nous
or Logos, the divine Intelligence, incarnate as they
had always believed in the whole world, and yet
truly the substance and essence of divinity. To
say that this incarnation had taken place pre-emi-
nently, or even exclusively, in Christ was not an
impossible concession to make to pious enthusiasm,
at least if the philosophy involved in the old conception could be retained and embodied in the
new orthodoxy. Sacred history could thus be interpreted as a temporal execution of eternal de-
crees, and the plan of salvation as an ideal necessity. Cosmic scope and metaphysical meaning
were given to Hebrew tenets, so unspeculative in
their original intention, and it became possible
even for a Platonic philosopher to declare himself
a Christian.

The eclectic Christian philosophy thus engen-
dered constitutes one of the most complete, elaborate, and impressive products of the
human mind. The ruins of more than
one civilisation and of more than one
philosophy were ransacked to furnish materials for
this heavenly Byzantium. It was a myth circum-
stantial and sober enough in tone to pass for an
account of facts, and yet loaded with enough miracle, poetry, and submerged wisdom to take the
place of a moral philosophy and present what
seemed at the time an adequate ideal to the heart.
Many a mortal, in all subsequent ages, perplexed

The resulting orthodox system.

and abandoned in this ungovernable world, has set sail resolutely for that enchanted island and found there a semblance of happiness, its narrow limits give so much room for the soul and its penitential soil breeds so many consolations. True, the brief time and narrow argument into which Christian imagination squeezes the world must seem to a speculative pantheist childish and poor, involving, as it does, a fatuous perversion of nature and history and a ridiculous emphasis laid on local events and partial interests. Yet just this violent reduction of things to a human stature, this half-innocent, half-arrogant assumption that what is important for a man must control the whole universe, is what made Christian philosophy originally appealing and what still arouses, in certain quarters, enthusiastic belief in its beneficence and finality.

Nor should we wonder at this enduring illusion. Man is still in his childhood; for he cannot respect an ideal which is not imposed on him against his will, nor can he find satisfaction in a good created by his own action. He is afraid of a universe that leaves him alone. Freedom appals him; he can apprehend in it nothing but tedium and desolation, so immature is he and so barren does he think himself to be. He has to imagine what the angels would say, so that his own good impulses (which create those angels) may gain in authority, and none of the dangers that surround his poor life make the least impression upon him until he

hears that there are hobgoblins hiding in the wood.
His moral life, to take shape at all, must appear
to him in fantastic symbols. The history of these
symbols is therefore the history of his soul.

There was in the beginning, so runs the Christian story, a great celestial King, wise and good,
The brief surrounded by a court of winged musi-
drama of cians and messengers. He had existed
things. from all eternity, but had always intended, when the right moment should come, to
create temporal beings, imperfect copies of himself in various degrees. These, of which man was
the chief, began their career in the year 4004 B. C.,
and they would live on an indefinite time, possibly,
that chronological symmetry might not be violated,
until A. D. 4004. The opening and close of this
drama were marked by two magnificent tableaux.
In the first, in obedience to the word of God, sun,
moon, and stars, and earth with all her plants and
animals, assumed their appropriate places, and nature sprang into being with all her laws. The first
man was made out of clay, by a special act of God,
and the first woman was fashioned from one of
his ribs, extracted while he lay in a deep sleep.
They were placed in an orchard where they often
could see God, its owner, walking in the cool of
the evening. He suffered them to range at will
and eat of all the fruits he had planted save that
of one tree only. But they, incited by a devil,
transgressed this single prohibition, and were ban-

ished from that paradise with a curse upon their head, the man to live by the sweat of his brow and the woman to bear children in labour. These children possessed from the moment of conception the inordinate natures which their parents had acquired. They were born to sin and to find disorder and death everywhere within and without them.

At the same time God, lest the work of his hands should wholly perish, promised to redeem in his good season some of Adam's children and restore them to a natural life. This redemption was to come ultimately through a descendant of Eve, whose foot should bruise the head of the serpent. But it was to be prefigured by many partial and special redemptions. Thus, Noah was to be saved from the deluge, Lot from Sodom, Isaac from the sacrifice, Moses from Egypt, the captive Jews from Babylon, and all faithful souls from heathen forgetfulness and idolatry. For a certain tribe had been set apart from the beginning to keep alive the memory of God's judgments and promises, while the rest of mankind, abandoned to its natural depravity, sank deeper and deeper into crimes and vanities. The deluge that came to punish these evils did not avail to cure them. "The world was renewed * and the earth rose again above the bosom of the waters, but in this renovation there remained eternally some trace of di-

* Bossuet : Discours sur l'histoire universelle, Part II, Chap. I.

vine vengeance. Until the deluge all nature had
been exceedingly hardy and vigorous, but by that
vast flood of water which God had spread out over
the earth, and by its long abiding there, all saps
were diluted; the air, charged with too dense and
heavy a moisture, bred ranker principles of corruption. The early constitution of the universe
was weakened, and human life, from stretching
as it had formerly done to near a thousand years,
grew gradually briefer. Herbs and roots lost their
primitive potency and stronger food had to be
furnished to man by the flesh of other animals.
. . . Death gained upon life and men felt themselves overtaken by a speedier chastisement. As
day by day they sank deeper in their wickedness, it
was but right they should daily, as it were, stick
faster in their woe. The very change in nourishment made manifest their decline and degradation,
since as they became feebler they became also more
voracious and blood-thirsty."

Henceforth there were two spirits, two parties,
or, as Saint Augustine called them, two cities in
the world. The City of Satan, whatever its arti-
fices in art, war, or philosophy, was essentially corrupt and impious. Its joy was but a comic mask
and its beauty the whitening of a sepulchre. It
stood condemned before God and before man's better conscience by its vanity, cruelty, and secret
misery, by its ignorance of all that it truly behoved a man to know who was destined to immortality. Lost, as it seemed, within this Babylon,

or visible only in its obscure and forgotten pur-
lieus, lived on at the same time the City of God,
the society of all the souls God predestined to
salvation; a city which, however humble and in-
conspicuous it might seem on earth, counted its
myriad transfigured citizens in heaven, and had
its destinies, like its foundations, in eternity. To
this City of God belonged, in the first place, the
patriarchs and the prophets who, throughout their
plaintive and ardent lives, were faithful to what
echoes still remained of a primeval revelation, and
waited patiently for the greater revelation to come.
To the same city belonged the magi who followed
a star till it halted over the stable in Bethlehem;
Simeon, who divined the present salvation of Israel; John the Baptist, who bore witness to the
same and made straight its path; and Peter, to
whom not flesh and blood, but the spirit of the
Father in heaven, revealed the Lord's divinity.
For salvation had indeed come with the fulness
of time, not, as the carnal Jews had imagined it,
in the form of an earthly restoration, but through
the incarnation of the Son of God in the Virgin
Mary, his death upon a cross, his descent into hell,
and his resurrection at the third day according to
the Scriptures. To the same city belonged finally
all those who, believing in the reality and efficacy
of Christ's mission, relied on his merits and followed his commandment of unearthly love.

All history was henceforth essentially nothing
but the conflict between these two cities; two mo-

ralities, one natural, the other supernatural; two philosophies, one rational, the other revealed; two beauties, one corporeal, the other spiritual; two glories, one temporal, the other eternal; two institutions, one the world, the other the Church. These, whatever their momentary alliances or compromises, were radically opposed and fundamentally alien to one another. Their conflict was to fill the ages until, when wheat and tares had long flourished together and exhausted between them the earth for whose substance they struggled, the harvest should come; the terrible day of reckoning when those who had believed the things of religion to be imaginary would behold with dismay the Lord visibly coming down through the clouds of heaven, the angels blowing their alarming trumpets, all generations of the dead rising from their graves, and judgment without appeal passed on every man, to the edification of the universal company and his own unspeakable joy or confusion. Whereupon the blessed would enter eternal bliss with God their master and the wicked everlasting torments with the devil whom they served.

The drama of history was thus to close upon a second tableau: long-robed and beatified cohorts passing above, amid various psalmodies, into an infinite luminous space, while below the damned, howling, writhing, and half transformed into loathsome beasts, should be engulfed in a fiery furnace. The two cities, always opposite in essence, should thus be finally divided in existence, each bearing its natural fruits and manifesting its true nature.

Let the reader fill out this outline for himself with its thousand details; let him remember the endless mysteries, arguments, martyrdoms, consecrations that carried out the sense and made vital the beauty of the whole. Let him pause before the phenomenon; he can ill afford, if he wishes to understand history or the human mind, to let the apparition float by unchallenged without delivering up its secret. What shall we say of this Christian dream?

Those who are still troubled by the fact that this dream is by many taken for a reality, and who are consequently obliged to defend themselves against it, as against some dangerous error in science or in philosophy, may be allowed to marshal arguments in its disproof. Such, however, is not my intention. Do we marshal arguments against the miraculous birth of Buddha, or the story of Cronos devouring his children? We seek rather to honour the piety and to understand the poetry embodied in those fables. If it be said that those fables are believed by no one, I reply that those fables are or have been believed just as unhesitatingly as the Christian theology, and by men no less reasonable or learned than the unhappy apologists of our own ancestral creeds. Matters of religion should never

Mythology is a language and must be understood to convey something by symbols.

be matters of controversy. We neither argue with
a lover about his taste, nor condemn him, if we
are just, for knowing so human a passion. That
he harbours it is no indication of a want of sanity
on his part in other matters. But while we acqui-
esce in his experience, and are glad he has it, we
need no arguments to dissuade us from sharing it.
Each man may have his own loves, but the object
in each case is different. And so it is, or should
be, in religion. Before the rise of those strange
and fraudulent Hebraic pretensions there was no
question among men about the national, personal,
and poetic character of religious allegiance. It
could never have been a duty to adopt a religion
not one's own any more than a language, a coin-
age, or a costume not current in one's own country. The idea that religion contains a literal, not
a symbolic, representation of truth and life is simply an impossible idea. Whoever entertains it has
not come within the region of profitable philoso-
phising on that subject. His science is not wide
enough to cover all existence. He has not discovered that there can be no moral allegiance except
to the ideal. His certitude and his arguments are
no more pertinent to the religious question than
would be the insults, blows, and murders to which,
if he could, he would appeal in the next instance.
Philosophy may describe unreason, as it may describe force; it cannot hope to refute them.

CHAPTER VII

PAGAN CUSTOM AND BARBARIAN GENIUS INFUSED INTO CHRISTIANITY

The western intellect, in order to accept the gospel, had to sublimate it into a neo-Platonic system of metaphysics. In like man-
Need of paganising Christianity. ner the western heart had to render Christianity congenial and adequate by a rich infusion of pagan custom and sentiment. This adaptation was more gentle and facile than might be supposed. We are too much inclined to impute an abstract and ideal Christianity to the polyglot souls of early Christians, and to ignore that mysterious and miraculous side of later paganism from which Christian cultus and ritual are chiefly derived. In the third century Christianity and devout paganism were, in a religious sense, closely akin; each differed much less from the other than from that religion which at other epochs had borne or should bear its own name. Had Julian the Apostate succeeded in his enterprise he would not have rescued anything which the admirers of classic paganism could at all rejoice in; a disciple of Iamblichus could not but plunge headlong into the same sea of superstition and dialectic which

had submerged Christianity. In both parties ethics were irrational and morals corrupt. The political and humane religion of antiquity had disappeared, and the question between Christians and pagans amounted simply to a choice of fanaticisms. Reason had suffered a general eclipse, but civilisation, although decayed, still subsisted, and a certain scholastic discipline, a certain speculative habit, and many an ancient religious usage remained in the world. The people could change their gods, but not the spirit in which they worshipped them. Christianity had insinuated itself almost unobserved into a society full of rooted traditions. The first disciples had been disinherited Jews, with religious habits which men of other races and interests could never have adopted intelligently; the Church was accordingly wise enough to perpetuate in its practice at least an indispensable minimum of popular paganism. How considerable this minimum was a glance at Catholic piety will suffice to convince us.

The Græco-Jewish system of theology constructed by the Fathers had its liturgical coun- Catholic piety more human than the liturgy. terpart in the sacraments and in a devout eloquence which may be represented to us fairly enough by the Roman missal and breviary. This liturgy, transfused as it is with pagan philosophy and removed thereby from the Oriental directness and formlessness of the Bible, keeps for the most part its theological and patristic tone. Psalms abound, Virgin and saints are barely mentioned, a certain universalism and concentration of thought upon the Redemption and its speculative meaning pervades the Latin ritual sung behind the altar-rails. But any one who enters a Catholic church with an intelligent interpreter will at once perceive the immense distance which separates that official and impersonal ritual from the daily prayers and practices of Catholic people. The latter refer to the real exigences of daily life and serve to express or re-organise personal passions. While mass is being celebrated the old woman will tell her beads, lost in a vague rumination over her own troubles; while the priests chant something unintelligible about Abraham or Nebuchadnezzar, the housewife will light her wax-candles, duly blessed for the occasion, before Saint Barbara, to be protected thereby from the lightning; and while the preacher is repeating, by rote, dialectical subtleties about the union of the two natures in Christ's person, a listener's fancy may float sadly over the mystery of love and of life, and (being himself without resources in the premises) he may order a mass to be said for the repose of some departed soul.

In a Catholic country, every spot and every man has a particular patron. These patrons are sometimes local worthies, canonised by tradition or by the Roman see, but no less often they are simply local appellations of Christ or the Virgin, appellations which are known theoretically to refer all to the same *numen*, but which practically possess diverse religious values; for the miracles and intercessions attributed to the Virgin under one title are far from being miracles and intercessions attributable to her under another. He who has been all his life devout to Loreto will not place any special reliance on the Pillar at Saragossa. A bereaved mother will not fly to the Immaculate Conception for comfort, but of course to Our Lady of the Seven Sorrows. Each religious order and all the laity more or less affiliated to it will cultivate special saints and special mysteries. There are also particular places and days on which graces are granted, as not on others, and the quantity of such graces is measurable by canonic standards. So many days of remitted penance correspond to a work of a certain merit, for there is a celestial currency in which mulcts and remissions may be accurately summed and subtracted by angelic recorders. One man's spiritual earnings may by gift be attributed and imputed to another, a belief which may seem arbitrary and superstitious but which is really a natural corollary to fundamental doctrines like the atonement, the communion of saints, and intercession for the dead and living.

Another phase of the same natural religion is seen in frequent festivals, in the consecration of **Natural** buildings, ships, fields, labours, and **pieties.** seasons; in intercessions by the greater dead for the living and by the living for the lesser dead—a perfect survival of heroes and penates on the one hand and of pagan funeral rites and commemorations on the other. Add Lent with its carnival, ember-days, all saints' and all souls', Christmas with its magi or its Saint Nicholas, Saint Agnes's and Saint Valentine's days with their profane associations, a saint for finding lost objects and another for prospering amourettes, since all great and tragic loves have their inevitable patrons in Christ and the Virgin, in Mary Magdalene, and in the mystics innumerable. This, with what more could easily be rehearsed, makes a complete paganism within Christian tradition, a paganism for which little basis can be found in the gospel, the mass, the breviary, or the theologians.

Yet these accretions were as well authenticated as the substructure, for they rested on human nature. To feel, for instance, the special efficacy of your village Virgin or of the miraculous Christ whose hermitage is perched on the overhanging hill, is a genuine experience. The principle of it is clear and simple. Those shrines, those images, the festivals associated with them, have entered your mind together with your earliest feelings. Your first glimpses of mortal vicissitudes have coincided with the awe and glitter of sacramental moments in which those *numina* were invoked; and on that deeper level of experience, in those lower reaches of irrationalism in which such impressions lie, they constitute a mystic resource subsisting beneath all conventions and overt knowledge. When the doctors blunder—as they commonly do—the saints may find a cure; after all, the saints' success in medicine seems to a crude empiricism almost as probable as the physicians'. Special and local patrons are the original gods, and whatever religious value speculative and cosmic deities retain they retain surreptitiously, by virtue of those very bonds with human interests and passionate desires which ancestral demons once borrowed from the hearth they guarded, the mountain they haunted, or the sacrifice they inhaled with pleasure, until their hearts softened toward their worshippers. In itself, and as a minimised and retreating theology represents it, a universal power has no specific energy, no determinate interest at heart; there is nothing friendly about it nor allied to your private necessities; no links of place and time fortify and define its influence. Nor is it rational to appeal for a mitigation of evils or for assistance against them to the very being that has decreed and is inflicting them for some fixed purpose of its own.

Paganism or natural religion was at first, like so many crude religious notions, optimistic and material; the worshipper expected his piety to make his pot boil, to cure his disease, to prosper his battles, and to render harmless his ignorance of the world in which he lived. But such faith ran up immediately against the facts; it was discountenanced at every turn by experience and reflection. The whole of nature and life, when they are understood at all, have to be understood on an opposite principle, on the principle that fate, having naturally furnished us with a determinate will and a determinate endowment, gives us a free field and no favour in a natural world. Hence the retreat of religion to the supernatural, a region to which in its cruder forms it was far from belonging. Now this retreat, in the case of classic paganism, took place with the decay of military and political life and would have produced an ascetic popular system, some compound of Oriental and Greek traditions, even if Christianity had not intervened at that juncture and opportunely pre-empted the ground.

Christianity, as we have seen, had elements in it which gave it a decisive advantage; its outlook was historical, not cosmic, and consequently admitted a non-natural future for the individual and for the Church; it was anti-political and looked for progress only in that region in which progress was at that time possible, in the private soul; it was democratic, feminine, and unworldly; its Oriental deity and prophets had a primitive simplicity and pathos not found in pagan heroes or polite metaphysical entities; its obscure Hebrew poetry opened, like music, an infinite field for brooding fancy and presumption. The consequence was a doubling of the world, so that every Christian led **The episodes** a dual existence, one full of trouble and **of life** vanity on earth, which it was piety in **consecrated** **mystically.** him to despise and neglect, another full of hope and consolation in a region parallel to earth and directly above it, every part of which

corresponded to something in earthly life and could
be reached, so to speak, by a Jacob's ladder upon
which aspiration and grace ascended and descended
continually. Birth had its sacramental consecration to the supernatural in baptism, growth in con-
firmation, self-consciousness in confession, puberty
in communion, effort in prayer, defeat in sacrifice,
sin in penance, speculation in revealed wisdom, art
in worship, natural kindness in charity, poverty in
humility, death in self-surrender and resurrection.
When the mind grew tired of contemplation the
lips could still echo some pious petition, keeping
the body's attitude and habit expressive of humility and propitious to receiving grace; and when
the knees and lips were themselves weary, a candle
might be left burning before the altar, to witness
that the desire momentarily forgotten was not extinguished in the heart. Through prayer and religious works the absent could be reached and the
dead helped on their journey, and amid earthly
estrangements and injustices there always remained
the church open to all and the society of heaven.

Nothing is accordingly more patent than that
Christianity was paganised by the early Church;
Paganism indeed, the creation of the Church was
chastened, itself what to a Hebraising mind must
Hebraism
liberalised. seem a corruption, namely, a mixing of
pagan philosophy and ritual with the Gospel. But
this sort of constitutive corruption would more
properly be called an adaptation, an absorption,
or even a civilisation of Hebraism; for by this mar-

riage with paganism Christianity fitted itself to live and work in the civilised world. By this corruption it was completed and immensely improved, like Anglo-Saxon by its corruption through French and Latin; for it is always an improvement in religion, whose business is to express and inspire spiritual sentiment, that it should learn to express and inspire that sentiment more generously. Paganism was nearer than Hebraism to the Life of Reason because its myths were more transparent and its temper less fanatical; and so a paganised Christianity approached more closely that ideality which constitutes religious truth than a bare and intense Hebraism, in its hostility to human genius, could ever have done if isolated and unqualified.

The Christianity which the pagans adopted, in becoming itself pagan, remained a religion natural to their country and their heart. It constituted a paganism expressive of their later and calamitous experience, a paganism acquainted with sorrow, a religion that had passed through both civilisation and despair, and had been reduced to translating the eclipsed values of life into supernatural symbols. It became a post-rational religion. Of course, to understand such a system it is necessary to possess the faculties it exercises and the experience it represents. Where life has not reached the level of reflection, religion and philosophy must both be pre-rational; they must remain crudely experimental, unconscious of the limits of excellence and

The system post-rational and founded on despair.

life. Under such circumstances it is obviously impossible that religion should be reconstituted on a supernatural plane, or should learn to express experience rather than impulse. Now the Christianity of the gospels was itself post-rational; it had turned its back on the world. In this respect the mixture with paganism altered nothing; it merely reinforced the spiritualised and lyric despair of the Hebrews with the personal and metaphysical despair of the Romans and Greeks. For all the later classic philosophy—Stoic, Sceptic, or Epicurean—was founded on despair and was postrational. Pagan Christianity, or Catholicism, may accordingly be said to consist of two elements: first, the genius of paganism, the faculty of expressing spiritual experience in myth and external symbol, and, second, the experience of disillusion, forcing that pagan imagination to take wing from earth and to decorate no longer the political and material circumstances of life, but rather to remove beyond the clouds and constitute its realm of spirit beyond the veil of time and nature, in a posthumous and metaphysical sphere. A mythical economy abounding in points of attachment to human experience and in genial interpretations of life, yet lifted beyond visible nature and filling a reported world, a world believed in on hearsay or, as it is called, on faith—that is Catholicism.

When this religion was established in the Roman Empire, that empire was itself threatened by the barbarians who soon permeated and occupied it and made a new and unhappy beginning to European history. They adopted Christianity, not because it represented their religious needs or inspiration, but because it formed part of a culture and a social organisation the influence of which they had not, in their simplicity, the means to withstand. During several ages they could only modify by their misunderstandings and inertia arts wholly new to their lives.

What sort of religion these barbarians may previously have had is beyond our accurate knowl-External con-edge. They handed down a mythology version of the not radically different from the Græco-barbarians. Roman, though more vaguely and grotesquely conceived; and they recognised tribal duties and glories from which religious sanctions could hardly have been absent. But a barbarian mind, like a child's, is easy to convert and to people with what stories you will. The Northmen drank in with pleased astonishment what the monks told them about hell and heaven, God the Father and God the Son, the Virgin and the beautiful angels; they accepted the sacraments with vague docility; they showed a qualified respect, often broken upon, it is true, by instinctive rebellions, for a clergy which after all represented whatever vestiges of learning, benevolence, or art still lingered in the world. But this easy and boasted conversion was fanciful only and skin-deep. A non-Christian ethics of valour and honour, a non-Christian fund of superstition, legend, and sentiment, subsisted always among mediæval peoples. Their soul, so largely inarticulate, might be overlaid with churchly habits and imprisoned for the moment in the panoply of patristic dogma; but pagan Christianity always remained a religion foreign to them, accepted only while their minds continued in a state of helpless tutelage. Such a foreign religion could never be understood by them in its genuine motives and spirit. They were without the experience and the plastic imagination which had given it birth. It might catch them unawares and prevail over them for a time, but even during that period it could not root out from barbarian souls anything opposed to it which subsisted there. It was thus that the Roman Church hatched the duck's egg of Protestantism.

In its native seats the Catholic system prompts among those who inwardly reject it satire and in-

Expression of the northern genius within Catholicism. difference rather than heresy, because on the whole it expresses well enough the religious instincts of the people. Only those strenuously oppose it who hate religion itself. But among converted barbarians the case was naturally different, and opposition to the Church came most vehemently from certain religious natures whose instincts it outraged or left unsatisfied. Even before heresy burst forth this religious restlessness found vent in many directions. It endowed Christianity with several beautiful but insidious gifts, several incongruous though well-meant forms of expression. Among these we may count Gothic art, chivalrous sentiment, and even scholastic philosophy. These things came, as we know, ostensibly to serve Christianity, which has learned to regard them as its own emanations. But in truth they barbarised Christianity just as Greek philosophy and worship and Roman habits of administration had paganised it in the beginning. And barbarised Christianity, even before it became heretical, was something new, something very different in temper and beauty from the pagan Christianity of the South and East.

In the Catholicism of the Middle Ages, as it flourished in the North, the barbarian soul, apprenticed to monkish masters, appeared in all its childlike trust, originality, and humour. There was something touching and grotesque about it. We seem to see a child playing with the toys of age, his green hopes and fancies weaving themselves about an antique metaphysical monument, the sanctuary of a decrepit world. The structure of that monument was at first not affected, and even when it had been undermined and partially ruined, its style could not be transformed, but, clad in its northern ivy, it wore at once a new aspect. To races without experience—that is, without cumulative traditions or a visible past—Christianity could be nothing but a fairy story and a gratuitous hope, as if they had been told about the Sultan of Timbuctoo and promised that they should some day ride on his winged Arabian horses. The tragic meaning of the Christian faith, its immense renunciation of all things earthly and the merely metaphysical glory of its transfigured life, commonly escaped their apprehension, as it still continues to do. They listened open-mouthed to the missionary and accepted his asseverations with unsuspecting emotion, like the Anglo-Saxon king who likened the soul to a bird flying in and out of a tent at night, about whose further fortunes any account would be interesting to hear. 'A seed planted in such a virgin and uncultivated soil must needs bring forth fruit of a new savour.

In northern Christianity a fresh quality of brooding tenderness prevailed over the tragic pas-

Internal discrepancies between the two.

sion elsewhere characteristic of Catholic devotion. Intricacy was substituted for dignity and poetry for rhetoric; the basilica became an abbey and the hermitage a school. The feudal ages were a wonderful seed-time in a world all gaunt with ruins. Horrors were there mingled with delicacies and confusion with idyllic peace. It was here a poet's childhood passed amid the crash of war, there an alchemist's old age flickering away amid cobwebs and gibberish. Something jocund and mischievous peeped out even in the cloister; gargoyles leered from the belfry, while ivy and holly grew about the cross. The Middle Ages were the true renaissance. Their Christianity was the theme, the occasion, the excuse for their art and jollity, their curiosity and tenderness; it was far from being the source of those delightful inventions. The Crusades were not inspired by the Prince of Peace, to whose honour they were fancifully and passionately dedicated; so chivalry, Gothic architecture, and scholastic philosophy were profane expressions of a self-discovering genius in a people incidentally Christian. The barbarians had indeed been indoctrinated, they had been introduced into an alien spiritual and historic medium, but they had not been made over or inwardly tamed. It had perhaps been rendered easier for them, by contact with an existing or remembered civilisation, to mature their own genius, even in the act of confusing its expression through foreign accretions. They had been thereby stimulated to civilise themselves and encouraged also to believe themselves civilised somewhat prematurely, when they had become heirs merely to the titles and trappings of civilisation.

The process of finding their own art and polity, begun under foreign guidance, was bound on the whole to diverge more and more from its Latin model. It consisted now of imitation, now of revulsion and fanciful originality; never was a race so much under the sway of fashions. Fashion is something barbarous, for it produces innovation without reason and imitation without benefit. It marks very clearly that margin of irresponsible variation in manners and thoughts which among a people artificially civilised may so easily be larger than the solid core.

It is characteristic of occidental society in mediæval and modern times, because this society is led
by people who, being educated in a foreign culture,
remain barbarians at heart. To this day we have
not achieved a really native civilisation. Our art,
morals, and religion, though deeply dyed in native
feeling, are still only definable and, indeed, conceivable by reference to classic and alien standards.
Among the northern races culture is even more
artificial and superinduced than among the southern; whence the strange phenomenon of snobbery
in society, affectation in art, and a violent contrast between the educated and the uneducated,
the rich and the poor, classes that live on different
intellectual planes and often have different religions. Some educated persons, accordingly, are
merely students and imbibers; they sit at the feet
of a past which, not being really theirs, can produce no fruit in them but sentimentality. Others
are merely *protestants;* they are active in the
moral sphere only by virtue of an inward rebellion
against something greater and overshadowing, yet
repulsive and alien. They are conscious truants
from a foreign school of life.

In the Protestant religion it is necessary to distinguish inner inspiration from historical entan-
Tradition   glements. Unfortunately, as the whole
and instinct   doctrinal form of this religion is irrele-
at odds in
Protestantism. vant to its spirit and imposed from
without, being due to the step-motherly nurture
it received from the Church, we can reach a con-

ception of its inner spirit only by studying its tendency and laws of change or its incidental expression in literature and custom. Yet these indirect symptoms are so striking that even an outsider, if at all observant, need not fear to misinterpret them. Taken externally, Protestantism is, of course, a form of Christianity; it retains the Bible and a more or less copious selection of patristic doctrines. But in its spirit and inward inspiration it is something quite as independent of Judea as of Rome. It is simply the natural religion of the Teutons raising its head above the flood of Roman and Judean influences. Its character may be indicated by saying that it is a religion of pure spontaneity, of emotional freedom, deeply respecting itself but scarcely deciphering its purposes. It is the self-consciousness of a spirit in process of incubation, jealous of its potentialities, averse to definitions and finalities of any kind because it can itself discern nothing fixed or final. It is adventurous and puzzled by the world, full of rudimentary virtues and clear fire, energetic, faithful, rebellious to experience, inexpert in all matters of art and mind. It boasts, not without cause, of its depth and purity; but this depth and purity are those of any formless and primordial substance. It keeps unsullied that antecedent integrity which is at the bottom of every living thing and at its core; it is not acquainted with that ulterior integrity, that sanctity, which might be attained at the summit of experience through reason and speculative dominion. It accordingly mistakes vitality, both in itself and in the universe, for spiritual life.

This underlying Teutonic religion, which we must call Protestantism for lack of a better name, is anterior to Christianity and can survive it. To identify it with the Gospel may have seemed possible so long as, in opposition to pagan Christianity, the Teutonic spirit could appeal to the Gospel for support. The Gospel has indeed nothing pagan about it, but it has also nothing Teutonic; and the momentary alliance of two such disparate forces must naturally cease with the removal of the common enemy which alone united them. The Gospel is unworldly, disenchanted, ascetic; it treats ecclesiastical establishments with tolerant contempt, conforming to them with indifference; it regards prosperity as a danger, earthly ties as a burden, Sabbaths as a superstition; it revels in miracles; it is democratic and antinomian; it loves contemplation, poverty, and solitude; it meets sinners with sympathy and heartfelt forgiveness, but Pharisees and Puritans with biting scorn. In a word, it is a product of the Orient, where all things are old and equal and a profound indifference to the business of earth breeds a silent dignity and high sadness in the spirit. Protestantism is the exact opposite of all this. It is convinced of the importance of success and prosperity; it abomi-

The Protestant spirit remote from that of the gospel.

nates what is disreputable; contemplation seems
to it idleness, solitude selfishness, and poverty a
sort of dishonourable punishment. It is con-
strained and punctilious in righteousness; it regards a married and industrious life as typically
godly, and there is a sacredness to it, as of a
vacant Sabbath, in the unoccupied higher spaces
which such an existence leaves for the soul. It
is sentimental, its ritual is meagre and unctuous,
it expects no miracles, it thinks optimism akin to
piety, and regards profitable enterprise and practical ambition as a sort of moral vocation. Its
Evangelicalism lacks the notes, so prominent in
the gospel, of disillusion, humility, and speculative detachment. Its benevolence is optimistic
and aims at raising men to a conventional well-
being; it thus misses the inner appeal of Christian charity which, being merely remedial in
physical matters, begins by renunciation and
looks to spiritual freedom and peace.

Protestantism was therefore attached from the
first to the Old Testament, in which Hebrew
fervour appears in its worldly and pre-rational
form. It is not democratic in the same sense as
post-rational religions, which see in the soul an
exile from some other sphere wearing for the
moment, perhaps, a beggar's disguise: it is democratic only in the sense of having a popular origin and bending easily to popular forces. Swayed
as it is by public opinion, it is necessarily conventional in its conception of duty and earnestly

materialistic; for the meaning of the word vanity never crosses the vulgar heart. In fine, it is the religion of a race young, wistful, and adventurous, feeling its latent potentialities, vaguely assured of an earthly vocation, and possessing, like the barbarian and the healthy child, pure but unchastened energies. Thus in the Protestant religion the faith natural to barbarism appears clothed, by force of historical accident, in the language of an adapted Christianity.

As the Middle Ages advanced the new-born human genius which constituted their culture

Obstacles to humanism.

grew daily more playful, curious, and ornate. It was naturally in the countries formerly pagan that this new paganism principally flourished. Religion began in certain quarters to be taken philosophically; its relation to life began to be understood, that it was a poetic expression of need, hope, and ignorance. Here prodigious vested interests and vested illusions of every sort made dangerous the path of sincerity. Genuine moral and religious impulses could not be easily dissociated from a system of thought and discipline with which for a thousand years they had been intimately interwoven. Scepticism, instead of seeming, what it naturally is, a moral force, a tendency to sincerity, economy, and fine adjustment of life and mind to experience—scepticism seemed a temptation and a danger. This situation, which still prevails in a certain measure, strikingly shows into how arti-

ficial a posture Christianity has thrown the mind.
If scepticism, under such circumstances, by
chance penetrated among the clergy, it was not
favourable to consistency of life, and it was the
more certain to penetrate among them in that
their ranks, in a fat and unscrupulous age, would
naturally be largely recruited by men without conscience or ideal ambitions. It became accordingly
necessary to reform something; either the gay
world to suit the Church's primitive austerity and
asceticism, or the Church to suit the world's profane and general interests. The latter task was
more or less consciously undertaken by the
humanists who would have abated the clergy's
wealth and irrational authority, advanced polite
learning, and, while of course retaining Christianity—for why should an ancestral religion be
changed?—would have retained it as a form of
paganism, as an ornament and poetic expression
of human life. This movement, had it not been
overwhelmed by the fanatical Reformation and
the fanatical reaction against it, would doubtless
have met with many a check from the Church's
sincere zealots; but it could have overcome them
and, had it been allowed to fight reason's battle
with reason's weapons, would ultimately have
led to general enlightenment without dividing
Christendom, kindling venomous religious and national passions, or vitiating philosophy.

It was not humanism, however, that was destined to restrain and soften the Church, com-

pleting by critical reflection that paganisation of
Christianity which had taken place at the begin-
The   ning instinctively and of necessity.
Reformation   There was now another force in the
and counter-
reformation.   field, the virgin conscience and wil-
fulness of the Teutonic races, sincerely attached
to what they had assimilated in Christianity
and now awakening to the fact that they inwardly abhorred and rejected the rest. This
situation, in so uncritical an age, could be interpreted as a return to primitive Christianity,
though this had been in truth, as we may now
perceive, utterly opposed to the Teutonic spirit.
Accordingly, the humanistic movement was
crossed and obscured by another, specifically
religious and ostensibly more Christian than the
Church. Controversies followed, as puerile as
they were bloody; for it was not to be expected
that the peoples once forming the Roman Empire were going to surrender their ancestral religion without a struggle and without resisting
this new barbarian invasion into their imagina-
tions and their souls. They might have suffered
their Christianised paganism to fade with time;
worldly prosperity and arts might have weaned
them gradually from their supernaturalism, and
science from their myths; but how were they to
abandon at once all their traditions, when challenged to do so by a foreign supernaturalism so
much poorer and cruder than their own? What
happened was that they intrenched themselves

in their system, cut themselves off from the genial influences that might have rendered it innocuous, and became sectaries, like their opponents. Enlightenment was only to come after a recrudescence of madness and by the mutual slaughter of a fresh crop of illusions, usurpations, and tyrannies.

It would be easy to write, in a satirical vein, the history of Protestant dogma. Its history was foreseen from the beginning by intelligent observers. It consisted in a gradual and inevitable descent into a pious scepticism. The attempt to cling to various intermediate positions on the inclined plane that slopes down from ancient revelation to private experience can succeed only for a time and where local influences limit speculative freedom. You must slide smilingly down to the bottom or, in horror at that eventuality, creep up again and reach out pathetically for a resting-place at the top. To insist on this rather obvious situation, as exhibited for instance in the Anglican Church, would be to thresh straw and to study in Protestantism only its feeble and accidental side. Its true essence is not constituted by the Christian dogmas that at a given moment it chances to retain, but by the spirit in which it constantly

Protestantism an expression of character, challenges the others, by the expression it gives to personal integrity, to faith in conscience, to human instinct courageously meeting the world. It rebels, for instance, against the Catholic system of measurable sins and merits, with rewards and punishments legally adjusted and controlled by priestly as well as by divine prerogative. Such a supernatural mechanism seems to an independent and uncowed nature a profanation and an imposture. Away, it says, with all intermediaries between the soul and God, with all meddlesome priestcraft and all mechanical salvation. Salvation shall be by faith alone, that is, by an attitude and sentiment private to the spirit, by an inner co-operation of man with the world. The Church shall be invisible, constituted by all those who possess this necessary faith and by no others. It really follows from this, although the conclusion may not be immediately drawn, that religion is not an adjustment to other facts or powers, or to other possibilities, than those met with in daily life and in surrounding nature, but is rather a spiritual adjustment to natural life, an insight into its principles, by which a man learns to identify himself with the cosmic power and to share its multifarious business no less than its ulterior security and calm.

Protestantism, in this perfectly instinctive trustfulness and self-assertion, is not only prior **It has the** to Christianity but more primitive **spirit of life,** than reason and even than man. The plants and animals, if they could speak, would express their attitude to their destiny in the Protestant fashion. " He that formed us," they would say, "lives and energises within us. He has sealed a covenant with us, to stand by us if we are faithful and strenuous in following the suggestions he whispers in our hearts. With fidelity to ourselves and, what is the same thing, to him, we are bound to prosper and to have life more and more abundantly for ever." This attitude, where it concerns religion, involves two corollaries: first, what in accordance with Hebrew precedent may be called symbolically faith in God, that is, confidence in one's own impulse and destiny, a confidence which the world in the end is sure to reward; and second, abomination of all contrary religious tenets and practices—of asceticism, for instance, because it denies the will; of idolatry and myth, because they render divinity concrete rather than relative to inner cravings and essentially responsive; finally of tradition and institutional authority, because these likewise jeopardise the soul's experimental development as, in profound isolation, she wrestles with reality and with her own inspiration.

In thus meeting the world the soul without experience shows a fine courage proportionate to
and of   its own vigour. We may well imagine
courage,   that lions and porpoises have a more masculine assurance that God is on their side than ever visits the breast of antelope or jellyfish. This assurance, when put to the test in adventurous living, becomes in a strong and

high-bred creature a refusal to be defeated, a
gallant determination to hold the last ditch and
hope for the best in spite of appearances. It
is a part of Protestantism to be austere, energetic, unwearied in some laborious task. The
end and profit are not so much regarded as the
mere habit of self-control and practical devotion
and steadiness. The point is to accomplish something, no matter particularly what; so that Protestants show on this ground some respect even
for an artist when he has once achieved success.
A certain experience of ill fortune is only a
stimulus to this fidelity. So great is the antecedent trust in the world that the world, as it
appears at first blush, may be confidently defied.

Hence, in spite of a theoretic optimism, disap-
proval and proscription play a large part in
Protestant sentiment. The zeal for righteousness, the practical expectation that all shall be
well, cannot tolerate recognised evils. Evils must
be abolished or at least hidden; they must not
offend the face of day and give the lie to
universal sanctimony. This austerity and re-
pression, though they involve occasional hypoc-
risy, lead also to substantial moral reconstruction. Protestantism, springing from a pure
heart, purifies convention and is a tonic to any
society in which it prominently exists. It has
the secret of that honest simplicity which belongs to unspoiled youth, that keen integrity
native to the ungalled spirit as yet unconscious

of any duplicity in itself or of any inward reason why it should fail. The only evils it recognises seem so many challenges to action, so many conditions for some glorious unthought-of victory. *but the voice of inexperience.* Such a religion is indeed profoundly ignorant, it is the religion of inexperience, yet it has, at its core, the very spirit of life. Its error is only to consider the will omnipotent and sacred and not to distinguish the fie'ld of inevitable failure from that of possible success. Success, however, would never be possible without that fund of energy and that latent resolve and determination which bring also faith in success. Animal optimism is a great renovator and disinfectant in the world.

It was this youthful religion—profound, barbaric, poetical—that the Teutonic races insin- *Its emancipation from Christianity.* uated into Christianity and substituted for that last sigh of two expiring worlds. In the end, with the complete crumbling away of Christian dogma and tradition, Absolute Egotism appeared openly on the surface in the shape of German speculative philosophy. This form, which Protestantism assumed at a moment of high tension and reckless self-sufficiency, it will doubtless shed in turn and take on new expressions; but that declaration of independence on the part of the Teutonic spirit marks emphatically its exit from Christianity and the end of that series of transformations in which it took the Bible and patristic dogma for its materials. It now bids fair to apply itself instead to social life and natural science and to attempt to feed its Protean hunger directly from these more homely sources.

CHAPTER VIII

CONFLICT OF MYTHOLOGY WITH MORAL TRUTH

That magic and mythology have no experimental sanction is clear so soon as experience **Myth should** begins to be gathered together with **dissolve with** **the advance** any care. As magic attempts to do **of science.** work by incantations, so myth tries to attain knowledge by playing with lies. The attempt is in the first instance inevitable and even innocent, for it takes time to discriminate valid from valueless fancies in a mind in which they spring up together, with no intrinsic mark to distinguish them. The idle notion attracts attention no less than the one destined to prove significant; often it pleases more. Only watchful eyes and that rare thing, conscience applied to memory, can pluck working notions from the gay and lascivious vegetation of the mind, or learn to prefer Cinderella to her impudent sisters. If a myth has some modicum of applicability or significance it takes root all the more firmly side by side with knowledge. There are many subjects of which man is naturally so ignorant that only mythical notions can seem to do them justice; such, for instance, are the

127

minds of other men.   Myth remains for this reason a constituent part even of the most rational consciousness, and what can at present be profitably attempted is not so much to abolish myth as to become aware of its mythical character.

The mark of a myth is that it does not interpret a phenomenon in terms capable of being subsumed under the same category with that phenomenon itself, but fills it out instead with images that could never appear side by side with it or complete it on its own plane of existence.   Thus if meditating on the moon I conceive her other side or the aspect she would wear if I were travelling on her surface, or the position she would assume in relation to the earth if viewed from some other planet, or the structure she would disclose could she be cut in halves, my thinking, however fanciful, would be on the scientific plane and not mythical, for it would forecast possible perceptions, complementary to those I am trying to enlarge.   If, on the other hand, I say the moon is the sun's sister, that she carries a silver bow, that she is a virgin and once looked lovingly on the sleeping Endymion, only the fool never knew it—my lucubration is mythical; for I do not pretend that this embroidery on the aspects which the moon actually wears in my feeling and in the interstices of my thoughts could ever be translated into perceptions making one system with the present image.   By going closer to that disc

I should not see the silver bow, nor by retreating in time should I come to the moment when the sun and moon were actually born of Latona. The elements are incongruous and do not form one existence but two, the first sensible, the other only to be enacted dramatically, and having at best to the first the relation of an experience to its symbol. These fancies are not foretastes of possible perceptions, but are free interpretations or translations of the perceptions I have actually had.

Mythical thinking has its roots in reality, but, like a plant, touches the ground only at one end. It stands unmoved and flowers wantonly into the air, transmuting into unexpected and richer forms the substances it sucks from the soil. It is therefore a fruit of experience, an ornament, a proof of animal vitality; but it is no *vehicle* for experience; it cannot serve the purposes of transitive thought or action. Science, on the other hand, is constituted by those fancies which, arising like myths out of perception, retain a sensuous language and point to further perceptions of the same kind; so that the suggestions drawn from one object perceived are only ideas of other objects similarly perceptible. A scientific hypothesis is one which represents something continuous with the observed facts and conceivably existent in the same medium. Science is a bridge touching experience at both ends, over which practical thought may travel from act to act, from perception to perception.

To separate fable from knowledge nothing is therefore requisite except close scrutiny and the principle of parsimony. Were mythology merely a poetic substitute for natural science the advance of science would sufficiently dispose of it. What remained over would, like the myths in Plato, be at least better than total silence on a subject that interests us and makes us think, although we have no means of testing our thoughts in its regard. But the chief source of perplexity and confusion in mythology is its confusion with moral truth. The myth which originally was but a symbol substituted for empirical descriptions becomes in the sequel an idol substituted for ideal values. This complication, from which half the troubles of philosophy arise, deserves our careful attention.

But myth is confused with the moral values it expresses.

European history has now come twice upon the dissolution of mythologies, first among the Stoics and then among the Protestants. The circumstances in the two cases were very unlike; so were the mythical systems that were discarded; and yet the issue was in both instances similar. Greek and Christian mythology have alike ended in pantheism. So soon as the constructions of the poets and the Fathers were seen to be ingenious fictions, criticism was confronted with an obvious duty: to break up the

mythical compound furnished by tradition into
its elements, putting on one side what natural
observation or actual history had supplied, and
on the other what dramatic imagination had
added. For a cool and disinterested observer the
task, where evidence and records were not wanting, would be simple enough. But the critic in
this case would not usually be cool or disinterested. His religion was concerned; he had no
other object to hang his faith and happiness
upon than just this traditional hybrid which his
own enlightenment was now dissolving. To which
part should he turn for support? In which quarter should he continue to place the object of his
worship?

From the age of the Sophists to the final disappearance of paganism nearly a thousand years
elapsed. A thousand years from the infliction
of a mortal wound to the moment of extinction
is a long agony. Religions do not disappear when
they are discredited; it is requisite that they
should be replaced. For a thousand years the
augurs may have laughed, they were bound
nevertheless to stand at their posts until the
monks came to relieve them. During this prolonged decrepitude paganism lived on inertia, by
accretions from the Orient, and by philosophic
reinterpretations. Of these reinterpretations the
Neo-Platonic first was that attempted by Plato,
revision. and afterward carried out by the
neo-Platonists and Christians into the notion of

a supernatural spiritual hierarchy; above, a dialectical deity, the hypostasis of intellect and its ontological phases; below, a host of angels and demons, hypostases of faculties, moral influences, and evil promptings. In other words, in the diremption of myths which yielded here a natural phenomenon to be explained and there a moral value to be embodied, Platonism attached divinity exclusively to the moral element. The ideas, which were essentially moral functions, were many and eternal; their physical embodiments were adventitious to them and constituted a lapse, a misfortune to be wiped out by an eventual reunion of the alienated nature with its own ideal. Religion in such a system necessarily meant redemption. In this movement paganism turned toward the future, toward supernatural and revealed religion, and away from its own naturalistic principle. Revelation, as Plato himself had said, was needed to guide a mind which distrusted phenomena and recoiled from earthly pursuits.

This religion had the strength of despair, but all else in it was weakness. Apart from a revelation which, until Christianity appeared, remained nebulous and arbitrary, there could be no means of maintaining the existence of those hypostasised moral entities. The effort to separate them from the natural functions which they evidently expressed could not succeed while any critical acumen or independence subsisted in the believer. Platonism, to become a re-

It made mythical entities of abstractions.

ligion, had to appeal to superstition. Unity, for instance (which, according to Plato himself, is a category applicable to everything concomitantly with the complementary category of multiplicity, for everything, he says, is evidently both one and many)—unity could not become the One, an independent and supreme deity, unless the meaning and function of unity were altogether forgotten and a foolish idolatry, agape at words, were substituted for understanding. Some one had to come with an air of authority and report his visions of the One before such an entity could be added to the catalogue of actual existences. The reality of all neo-Platonic hypostasis was thus dependent on revelation and on forgetting the meaning once conveyed by the terms so mysteriously transfigured into metaphysical beings.

This divorce of neo-Platonic ideas from the functions they originally represented in human life and discourse was found in the end to defeat the very interest that had prompted it—enthusiasm for the ideal. Enthusiasm for the ideal had led Plato to treat all beauties as stepping-stones toward a perfect beauty in which all their charms might be present together, eternally and without alloy. Enthusiasm for the ideal had persuaded him that mortal life was only an impeded effort to fall back into eternity. These inspired but strictly unthinkable suggestions fell from his lips in his zeal to express how much the burden and import of experience exceeded its sensuous vehicle in permanence and value. A thousand triangles revealed one pregnant proportion of lines and areas; a thousand beds and bridles served one perpetual purpose in human life, and found in fulfilling it their essence and standard of excellence; a thousand fascinations taught the same lesson and coalesced into one reverent devotion to beauty and nobility wherever they might bloom. It was accordingly a poignant sense for the excellence of real things that made Plato wish to transcend them; his metaphysics was nothing but a visionary intuition of values, an idealism in the proper sense of the word. But when the momentum of such enthusiasm remained without its motive power, and its transcendence without its inspiration in real experience, idealism ceased to be an idealisation, an interpretation of reality reaching prophet-

Hypostasis ruins ideals. ically to its goals. It became a supernumerary second physics, a world to which an existence was attributed which could be hardly conceived and was certainly supported by no evidence, while that significance which it really possessed in reference to natural processes was ignored, or even denied. An idealism which had consisted in understanding and discriminating values now became a superstition incapable of discerning existences. It added a prodigious fictitious setting to the cosmos in which man had to operate; it obscured his real interests and possible happiness by seeking to transport him into that unreal environment, with its fantastic and disproportionate economy; and, worst of all, it robbed the ideal of its ideality by tearing it up from its roots in natural will and in experienced earthly benefits. For an ideal is not ideal if it is the ideal of nothing. In that case it is only a ghostly existence, with no more moral significance or authority in relation to the observer than has any happy creature which may happen to exist somewhere in the unknown reaches of the universe.

Meantime, a second reinterpretation of mythology was attempted by the Stoics. Instead of moving forward, like Plato, toward the supernaturalism that was for so many ages to dominate the world, the Stoics, with greater loyalty to pagan principles, reverted to the natural forces that had been the chief basis for the traditional deities. The progress of philosophy had given the Stoics a notion of the cosmos such as the early Aryan could not have possessed when he recorded and took to heart his scattered observations in the form of divine influences, as many and various as the observations themselves. To the Stoics the world was evidently one dynamic system. The power that animated it was therefore one God. Accordingly, after explaining away the popular myths by turning them somewhat ruthlessly into moral apologues, they proceeded to identify Zeus with the order of nature. This identification was supported by many traditional tendencies and philosophic hints. The resulting concept, though still mythical, was perhaps as rationalistic as the state of science at the time could allow. Zeus had been from the beginning a natural force, at once serene and formidable, the thunderer no less than the spirit of the blue. He was the ruler of gods and men; he was, under limitations, a sort of general providence. Anaxagoras, too, in proclaiming the cosmic function of reason, had prepared the way for the Stoics in another direction. This "reason," which in Socrates and Plato was already a deity, meant an order, an order making for the good. It was the name for a principle much like that which Aristotle called Nature, an indwelling prophetic instinct by which things strive after their perfection and happiness. Now Aristotle observed this instinct, as behoved a disciple of Socrates, in its specific cases, in which the good secured could be discriminated and visibly attained. There were many souls, each with its provident function and immutable guiding ideal, one for each man and animal, one for each heavenly sphere, and one, the prime mover, for the highest sphere of all. But the Stoics, not trained in the same humane and critical school, had felt the unity of things more dramatically and vaguely in the realm of physics. Like Xenophanes of old, they gazed at the broad sky and exclaimed, "The All is One." Uniting these various influences, they found it easy to frame a conception of Zeus, or the world, or the universal justice and law, so as to combine in it a dynamic unity with a provident reason. A world conceived to be material

and fatally determined was endowed with foresight of its own changes, perfect internal harmony,
and absolute moral dignity. Thus mythology, with
the Stoics, ended in pantheism.

By reducing their gods to a single divine influence, and identifying this in turn with natural
forces, the Stoics had, in one sense, saved mythology. For no one would be inclined to deny existence or power to the cosmos, to the body the
soul of which was Zeus. Pantheism, taken theoretically, is only naturalism poetically expressed.
It therefore was a most legitimate and congenial
interpretation of paganism for a rationalistic age.
On the other hand, mythology had not been a
mere poetic physics; it had formulated the object
of religion; it had embodied for mankind its highest ideals in worshipful forms. It was when this
religious function was transferred to the god of
The ideal   pantheism that the paradox and im-
surrendered
before the   possibility of the reform became evi-
physical.   dent. Nature neither is nor can be
man's ideal. The substitution of nature for the
traditional and ideal object of religion involves
giving nature moral authority over man; it involves that element of Stoicism which is the syno-
nym of inhumanity. Life and death, good and
ill fortune, happiness and misery, since they flow
equally from the universal order, shall be declared,
in spite of reason, to be equally good. True virtue
shall be reduced to conformity. He who has no
ideal but that nature should possess her actual

constitution will be wise and superior to all flattery and calamity; he will be equal in dignity to Zeus. He who has any less conformable and more determinate interests will be a fool and a worm.

The wise man will, meantime, perform all the offices of nature; he will lend his body and his mind to her predestined labours. For pantheistic morals, though post-rational, are not ascetic. In dislodging the natural ideal from the mind, they put in its place not its supernatural exaggeration but a curtailment of it inspired by despair. The passions are not renounced on the ground that they impede salvation or some visionary ecstasy; they are merely chilled by the sense that their defeat, when actual, is also desirable. As all the gods have been reduced to one substance or law, so all human treasures are reduced to one privilege—that of fortitude. You can always consent, and by a forced and perpetual conformity to nature lift yourself above all vicissitudes. Those tender and tentative ideals which nature really breeds, and which fill her with imperfect but genuine excellences, you will be too stolid to perceive or too proud to share.

Thus the hereditary taint of mythology, the poison of lies, survived in the two forms of philosophic paganism which it concerns us to study. In Plato's school, myth helped to hypostasise the ideas and, by divorcing them from their natural basis, to deprive them of their significance and moral function, and render the worship of them

superstitious. In the Stoa the surviving mythological element turned nature, when her unity and
order had been perceived, into an idol; so that the
worship of her blasted all humane and plastic
ideals and set men upon a vain and fanatical self-
denial. Both philosophies were post-rational, as
befitted a decadent age and as their rival and heir,
Christianity, was also.

Christianity had already within itself a similar
duality; being a doctrine of redemption, like neo-
Platonism, it tended to deny the natural values of this life; but, being a
doctrine of creation and providential
government, comparable in a way to the Stoic, it
had an ineradicable inward tendency toward pantheism, and toward a consequent acceptance of
both the goods and evils of this world as sanctioned
and required by providence.

The horror which pantheism has always inspired
in the Church is like that which materialism inspires in sentimental idealists; they attack it continually, not so much because
anybody else defends it as because they
feel it to be implied unmistakably in half their
own tenets. The non-Platonic half of Christian
theology, the Mosaic half, is bound to become pantheism in the hands of a philosopher. The Jews
were not pantheists themselves, because they never
speculated on the relation which omnipotence
stood in to natural forces and human acts. They
conceived Jehovah's omnipotence dramatically, as

*Parallel
movements in
Christianity.*

*Hebraism, if
philosophical,
must be
pantheistic.*

they conceived everything. He might pounce upon
anything and anybody; he might subvert or play
with the laws of nature; he might laugh at men's
devices, and turn them to his own ends; his craft
and energy could not but succeed in every instance; but that was not to say that men and
nature had no will of their own, and did not proceed naturally on their respective ways when Jehovah happened to be busy elsewhere. So soon,
however, as this dramatic sort of omnipotence was
made systematic by dialectic, so soon as the doctrines of creation, omniscience, and providential
government were taken absolutely, pantheism was
clearly involved. The consequences to moral philosophy were truly appalling, for then the sins
God punished so signally were due to his own con-
trivance. The fervours of his saints, the fate of
his chosen people and holy temples, became nothing but a puppet-show in his ironical self-consciousness.

The strangest part of this system, or what would
seem so if its antecedents were not known, is that
Pantheism, it is only half-conscious of its physical
even when
psychic, temper, and in calling itself an idealism
ignores ideals. (because it makes perception and will
the substance of their objects), thinks itself an
expression of human aspirations. This illusion
has deep historical roots. It is the last stage of
a mythical philosophy which has been earnestly
criticising its metaphors, on the assumption that
they were not metaphorical; whereby it has stripped

them of all significance and reduced them at last
to the bare principle of inversion. Nothing is any
longer idealised, yet all is still called an idealism.
A myth is an inverted image of things, wherein
their moral effects are turned into their dramatic
antecedents—as when the wind's rudeness is
turned into his anger. When the natural basis
of moral life is not understood, myth is the only
way of expressing it theoretically, as eyes too weak
to see the sun face to face may, as Plato says, for
a time study its image mirrored in pools, and, as
we may add, inverted there. So the good, which
in itself is spiritual only, is transposed into a natural power. At first this amounts to an amiable
misrepresentation of natural things; the gods in-
habit Mount Olympus and the Elysian Fields are
not far west of Cadiz. With the advance of geography the mythical facts recede, and in a cosmography like Hegel's, for instance, they have disappeared altogether; but there remain the mythical
values once ascribed to those ideal objects but now
transferred and fettered to the sad realities that
have appeared in their place. The titles of honour once bestowed on a fabled world are thus
applied to the real world by right of inheritance.

Nothing could be clearer than the grounds on
Truly divine which pious men in the beginning rec-
action ognise divine agencies. We see, they
limited to say, the hand of God in our lives. He
what makes
for the good. has saved us from dangers, he has com-
forted us in sorrow. He has blessed us with the

treasures of life, of intelligence, of affection. He
has set around us a beautiful world, and one still
more beautiful within us. Pondering all these
blessings, we are convinced that he is mighty in
the world and will know how to make all things
good to those who trust in him. In other words,
pious men discern God in the excellence of things.
If all were well, as they hope it may some day be,
God would henceforth be present in everything.
While good is mixed with evil, he is active in the
good alone. The pleasantness of life, the precious-
ness of human possessions, the beauty and promise
of the world, are proof of God's power; so is the
stilling of tempests and the forgiveness of sins.
But the sin itself and the tempest, which optimistic theology has to attribute just as much to God's
purposes, are not attributed to him at all by pious
feeling, but rather to his enemies. In spite of
centuries wasted in preaching God's omnipotence,
his omnipotence is contradicted by every Christian
judgment and every Christian prayer. If the most
pious of nations is engaged in war, and suffers a
great accidental disaster, such as it might expect
to be safe from, *Te deums* are sung for those that
were saved and *Requiems* for those that perished.
God's office, in both cases, is to save only. No one
seriously imagines that Providence does more
than *govern*—that is, watch over and incidentally
modify the natural course of affairs—not even in
the other world, if fortunes are still changeable
there.

The criterion of divine activity could not be placed more squarely and unequivocally in the good. Plato and Aristotle are not in this respect better moralists than is an unsophisticated piety. God is the ideal, and what manifests the ideal manifests God. Are you confident of the permanence and triumph of the things you prize? Then you trust in God, you live in the consciousness of his presence. The proof and measure of rationality in the world, and of God's power over it, is the extent of human satisfactions. In hell, good people would disbelieve in God, and it is impious of the trembling devils to believe in him there.

Need of an opposing principle. The existence of any evil—and if evil is felt it exists, for experience is its locus—is a proof that some accident has intruded into God's works. If that loyalty to the good, which is the prerequisite of rationality, is to remain standing, we must admit into the world, while it contains anything practically evil, a principle, however minimised, which is not rational. This irrational principle may be inertia in matter, accidental perversity in the will, or ultimate conflict of interests. Somehow an element of resistance to the rational order must be introduced somewhere. And immediately, in order to distinguish the part furnished by reason from its irrational alloy, we must find some practical test; for if we are to show that there is a great and triumphant rationality in the world, in spite of irrational accidents and brute opposition, we must frame an idea of rationality different from that of being. It will no longer do to say, with the optimists, the rational is the real, the real is the rational. For we wish to make a distinction, in order to maintain our loyalty to the good, and not to eviscerate the idea of reason by emptying it of its essential meaning, which is action addressed to the good and thought envisaging the ideal. To pious feeling, the free-will of creatures, their power, active or passive, of independent origination, is the explanation of all defects; and everything which is not helpful to men's purposes must be assigned to their own irrationality as its cause. Herein lies the explanation of that paradox in religious feeling which attributes sin to the free will, but repentance and every good work to divine grace. Physically considered—as theology must consider the matter—both acts and both volitions are equally necessary and involved in the universal order; but practical religion calls divine only what makes for the good. Whence it follows at once that, both within and without us, what is done well is God's doing, and what is done ill is not.

Thus what we may call the practical or Hebrew theory of cosmic rationality betrays in plainest possible manner that reason is primarily a function of human nature. Reason dwells in the world in so far as the world is good, and the world is good in so far as it supports the wills it generates—the excellence

The standard of value is human.

of each creature, the value of its life, and the satisfaction of its ultimate desires. Thus Hebrew optimism could be moral because, although it asserted in a sense the morality of the universe, it asserted this only by virtue of a belief that the universe supported human ideals. Undoubtedly much insistence on the greatness of that power which made for righteousness was in danger of passing over into idolatry of greatness and power, for whatever they may make. Yet these relapses into Nature-worship are the more rare in that the Jews were not a speculative people, and had in the end to endow even Job with his worldly goods in order to rationalise his constancy. It was only by a scandalous heresy that Spinoza could so change the idea of God as to make him indifferent to his creatures; and this transformation, in spite of the mystic and stoical piety of its author, passed very justly for atheism; for that divine government and policy had been denied by which alone God was made manifest to the Hebrews.

If Job's reward seems to us unworthy, we must remember that we have since passed through the discipline of an extreme moral idealism, through a religion of sacrifice and sorrow. We should not confuse the principle that virtue must somehow secure the highest good (for what should not secure it would not be virtue) with the gross symbols by which the highest good might be expressed at Jerusalem. That Job should recover a thousand she-asses may seem to us a poor sop for his long anguish of mind and body, and we may hardly agree with him in finding his new set of children just as good as the old. Yet if fidelity had led to no good end, if it had not somehow brought happiness to somebody, that fidelity would have been folly. There is a noble folly which consists in pushing a principle usually beneficent to such lengths as to render it pernicious; and the pertinacity of Job would have been a case of such noble folly if we were not somehow assured of its ultimate fruits. In Christianity we have the same principle, save that the fruits of virtue are more spiritually conceived; they are inward peace, the silence of the passions, the possession of truth, and the love of God and of our fellows. This is a different conception of happiness, incomplete, perhaps, in a different direction. But were even this attenuated happiness impossible to realise, all rationality would vanish not merely from Christian charity and discipline, but from the whole Christian theory of creation, redemption, and judgment. Without some window open to heaven, religion would be more fantastic than worldliness without being less irrational and vain.

Revelation has intervened to bring about a conception of the highest good which never could have been derived from an impartial synthesis of human interests. The influence of great personalities and the fanaticism of peculiar times and races have joined in imposing such variations from the natural ideal. The rationality of the world, as Christianity conceived it, is due to the plan of salvation; and the satisfaction of human nature, **Hope for happiness makes belief in God.** however purified and developed, is what salvation means. If an ascetic ideal could for a moment seem acceptable, it was because the decadence and sophistication of the world had produced a great despair in all noble minds; and they thought it better that an eye or a hand which had offended should perish, and that they should enter blind and maimed into the kingdom of heaven, than that, whole and seeing, they should remain for ever in hell-fire. Supernatural, then, as the ideal might seem, and imposed on human nature from above, it was yet accepted only because nothing else, in that state of conscience and imagination, could revive hope; nothing else seemed to offer an escape from the heart's corruption and weariness into a new existence.

CHAPTER IX

THE CHRISTIAN COMPROMISE

The human spirit has not passed in historical times through a more critical situation or a greater revulsion than that involved in accepting Christianity. Was this event favourable to the Life of Reason? Was it a progress in competence, understanding, and happiness? Any absolute answer would be misleading. Christianity did not come to destroy; the ancient springs were dry already, and for two or three centuries unmistakable signs of decadence had appeared in every sphere, not least in that of religion and philosophy. Christianity was a reconstruction out of ruins. In the new world competence could only be indirect, understanding mythical, happiness surreptitious; but all three subsisted, and it was Christianity that gave them their necessary disguises.

The young West had failed in its first great experiment, for, though classic virtue and beauty and a great classic state subsisted, the force that had created them was spent. Was it possible to try again? Was it necessary to sit down, like the Orient, in perpetual flux and eternal apathy? This question was an-

Suspense between hope and disillusion.

148

swered by Christianity in a way, under the circumstances, extremely happy. The Gospel, on which Christianity was founded, had drawn a very sharp contrast between this world and the kingdom of heaven—a phrase admitting many interpretations. From the Jewish millennium or a celestial paradise it could shift its sense to mean the invisible Church, or even the inner life of each mystical spirit. Platonic philosophy, to which patristic theology was allied, had made a contrast not less extreme between sense and spirit, between life in time and absorption in eternity. Armed with this double dualism, Christianity could preach both renunciation and hope, both asceticism and action. both the misery of life and the blessing of creation. It even enshrined the two attitudes in its dogma, uniting the Jewish doctrine of a divine Creator and Governor of this world with that of a divine Redeemer to lead us into another. Persons were not lacking to perceive the contradiction inherent in such an eclecticism; and it was the Gnostic or neo-Platonic party, which denied creation and taught a pure asceticism, that had the best of the argument. The West, however, would not yield to their logic. It might, in an hour of trouble and weakness, make concessions to quietism and accept the cross, but it would not suffer the naturalistic note to die out altogether. It preferred an inconsistency, which it hardly perceived, to a complete surrender of its instincts. It settled down to the conviction that God created the world *and* redeemed it; that the soul is naturally good *and* needs salvation.

This contradiction can be explained exoterically by saying that time and changed circumstances **Superficial** separate the two situations: having **solution.** made the world perfect, God redeems it after it has become corrupt; and whereas all things are naturally good, they may by accident lose their excellence, and need to have it restored. There is, however, an esoteric side to the matter. A soul that may be redeemed, a will that may look forward to a situation in which its action will not be vain or sinful, is one that in truth has never sinned; it has merely been thwarted. Its ambition is rational, and what its heart desires is essentially good and ideal. So that the whole classic attitude, the faith in action, art, and intellect, is preserved under this protecting cuticle of dogma; nothing was needed but a little courage, and circumstances somewhat more favourable, for the natural man to assert himself again. A people believing in the resurrection of the flesh in heaven will not be averse to a reawakening of the mind on earth.

Another pitfall, however, opens here. These contrasted doctrines may change rôles. So long **But from** as by redemption we understand, in the **what shall** mystic way, exaltation above finitude **we be** **redeemed?** and existence, because all particularity is sin, to be redeemed is to abandon the Life of Reason; but redemption might mean extrication from untoward accidents, so that a rational life might be led under right conditions. Instead of being like Buddha, the redeemer might be like Prometheus. In that case, however, the creator would become like Zeus—a tyrant will responsible for our conditions rather than expressive of our ideal. The doctrine of creation would become pantheism and that of redemption, formerly ascetic, would represent struggling humanity.

The seething of these potent and ambiguous elements can be studied nowhere better than in Saint Augustine. He is a more genial and complete representative of Christianity than any of the Greek Fathers, in whom the Hebraic and Roman vitality was comparatively absent. Philosophy was only one phase of Augustine's genius; with him it was an instrument of zeal and a stepping-stone to salvation. Scarcely had it been born out of rhetoric when it was smothered in authority. Yet even in that precarious and episodic form it acquired a wonderful sweep, depth, and technical elaboration. He stands at the watershed of history, looking over either land; his invectives teach us almost as much of paganism and heresy as his exhortations do of Catholicism. To Greek subtlety he joins Hebrew fervour and monkish intolerance; he has a Latin amplitude and (it must be confessed) coarseness of feeling; but above all he is the illumined, enraptured, forgiven saint. In him theology, however speculative, remains a vehicle for living piety; and while he has, perhaps, done more than any

Typical attitude of St. Augustine.

other man to materialise Christianity, no one was ever more truly filled with its spirit.

Saint Augustine was a thorough Platonist, but to reach that position he had to pass in his youth through severe mental struggles. The difficult triumph over the sensuous imagination by which he attained the conception of intelligible objects was won only after long discipline and much reading of Platonising philosophers. Every reality seemed to him at first an object of sense: God, if he existed, must be perceptible, for to Saint Augustine's mind also, at this early and sensuous stage of its development, *esse* was *percipi*. He might never have worked himself loose from these limitations, with which his vivid fancy and not too delicate eloquence might easily have been satisfied, had it not been for his preoccupation with theology. God must somehow be conceived; for no one in that age of religious need and of theological passion felt both more intensely than Saint Augustine. If sensible objects alone were real, God must be somewhere discoverable in space; he must either have a body like the human, or be the body of the universe, or some subtler body permeating and moving all the rest.

These conceptions all offered serious dialectical difficulties, and, what was more to the point, they did not satisfy the religious and idealistic instinct which the whole movement of Saint Augustine's mind obeyed. So he pressed his inquiries farther. At length meditation, and more, perhaps, that

He achieves Platonism.

experience of the flux and vanity of natural things
on which Plato himself had built his heaven of
ideas, persuaded him that reality and substantial-
ity, in any eulogistic sense, must belong rather to
the imperceptible and eternal.   Only that which is
never an object of sense or experience can be the
root and principle of experience and sense.   Only
the invisible and changeless can be the substance
of a moving show.   God could now be apprehended
and believed in precisely because he was essentially
invisible: had he anywhere appeared he could not
be the principle of all appearance; had he had a
body and a *locus* in the universe, he could not have
been its spiritual creator.   The ultimate objects
of human knowledge were accordingly ideas, not
things; principles reached by the intellect, not objects by any possibility offered to sense.   The
methodological concepts of science, by which we
pass from fact to fact and from past perception
to future, did not attract Augustine's attention.
He admitted, it is true, that there was a subordinate, and to him apparently uninteresting, region
governed by " *certissima ratione vel experientia,*"
and he even wished science to be allowed a free
hand within that empirical and logical sphere.   A
mystic and allegorical interpretation of Scripture
was to be invoked to avoid the puerilities into
which any literal interpretation—of the creation
in six days, for instance—would be sure to run.
Unbelievers would thus not be scandalised by
mythical dogmas " concerning things which they

might have actually experienced, or discovered by
sure calculation."

Science was to have its way in the field of calculable experience; that region could be the more
readily surrendered by Augustine because his attention was henceforth held by those ideal objects
which he had so laboriously come to conceive.
These were concepts of the contemplative reason
or imagination, which envisages natures and eternal essences behind the variations of experience,
essences which at first receive names, becoming
thus the centres of rational discourse, then acquire
values, becoming guides to action and measures
of achievement, and finally attract unconditional
worship, being regarded as the first causes and
ultimate goals of all existence and aspiration.

This purely Platonic philosophy, however, was
not to stand alone. Like every phase of Saint
Augustine's speculation, it came, as we
have said, to buttress or express some
religious belief. But it is a proof of
his depth and purity of soul that his searching
philosophic intuition did more to spiritualise the
dogmas he accepted from others than these dogmas could do to denaturalise his spontaneous
philosophy. Platonic ideas had by that time long
lost their moral and representative value, their
Socratic significance. They had become ontological entities, whereas originally they had represented the rational functions of life. This
hypostasis of the rational, by which the rational

He identifies
it with
Christianity.

abdicates its meaning in the effort to acquire a
metaphysical existence, had already been carried
to its extreme by the Neo-Platonists. But Saint
Augustine, while helpless as a philosopher to resist that speculative realism, was able as a Christian
to infuse into those dead concepts some of the
human blood which had originally quickened them.
Metaphysics had turned all human interests into
mythical beings, and now religion, without at all
condemning o̒r understanding that transformation,
was going to adopt those mythical beings and turn
them again into moral influences. In Saint Augustine's mind, fed as it was by the Psalmist, the
Platonic figments became the Christian God, the
Christian Church, and the Christian soul, and thus
acquired an even subtler moral fragrance than that
which they had lost when they were uprooted by
a visionary philosophy from the soil of Greek culture.

Saint Augustine's way of conceiving God is an
excellent illustration of the power, inherent in his
God the religious genius and sincerity, of giving
good. life and validity to ideas which he was
obliged to borrow in part from a fabulous tradition
and in part from a petrified metaphysics. God,
to him, was simply the ideal eternal object of
human thought and love. All ideation on an intellectual plane was a vague perception of the divine essence. "The rational soul understands
God, for it understands what exists always unchanged." . . . "God is happiness; and in him

and from him and through him all things are
happy which are happy at all.   God is the good
and the beautiful." He was never tired of telling
us that God is not true but the truth (*i. e.,* the
ideal object of thought in any sphere), not good
but the good (*i. e.,* the ideal object of will in all
its rational manifestations).   In other words, whenever a man, reflecting on his experience, conceived
the better or the best, the perfect and the eternal,
he conceived God, inadequately, of course, yet essentially, because God signified the comprehensive
ideal of all the perfections which the human spirit
could behold in itself or in its objects.   Of this
divine essence, accordingly, every interesting thing
was a manifestation; all virtue and beauty were
parcels of it, tokens of its superabundant grace.
Hence the inexhaustible passion of Saint Augustine
toward his God; hence the sweetness of that endless colloquy in prayer into which he was continually relapsing, a passion and a sweetness which no
one will understand to whom God is primarily a
natural power and only accidentally a moral ideal.

Herein lies the chief difference between those in
whom religion is spontaneous and primary—a very
few—and those in whom it is imitative
and secondary.   To the former, divine
things are inward values, projected by
chance into images furnished by poetic tradition
or by external nature, while to the latter, divine
things are in the first instance objective factors of
nature or of social tradition, although they have

Primary and
secondary
religion.

come, perhaps, to possess some point of contact
with the interests of the inner life on account of
the supposed physical influence which those superhuman entities have over human fortunes. In a
word, theology, for those whose religion is secondary, is simply a false physics, a doctrine about
eventual experience not founded on the experience
of the past. Such a false physics, however, is soon
discredited by events; it does not require much
experience or much shrewdness to discover that
supernatural beings and laws are without the empirical efficacy which was attributed to them.
True physics and true history must always tend,
in enlightened minds, to supplant those misinter-
preted religious traditions. Therefore, those whose
reflection or sentiment does not furnish them with
a key to the moral symbolism and poetic validity
underlying theological ideas, if they apply their
intelligence to the subject at all, and care to be
sincere, will very soon come to regard religion as
a delusion. Where religion is primary, however,
all that worldly dread of fraud and illusion becomes irrelevant, as it is irrelevant to an artist's
pleasure to be warned that the beauty he expresses
has no objective existence, or as it would be irrelevant to a mathematician's reasoning to suspect that
Pythagoras was a myth and his supposed philosophy an abracadabra. To the religious man religion
is inwardly justified. God has no need of natural
or logical witnesses, but speaks himself within the
heart, being indeed that ineffable attraction which

dwells in whatever is good and beautiful, and that
persuasive visitation of the soul by the eternal and
incorruptible by which she feels herself purified,
rescued from mortality, and given an inheritance
in the truth. This is precisely what Saint Augustine knew and felt with remarkable clearness and
persistence, and what he expressed unmistakably
by saying that every intellectual perception is
knowledge of God or has God's nature for its object.

Proofs of the existence of God are therefore
not needed, since his existence is in one sense obvious and in another of no religious interest. It
is obvious in the sense that the ideal is a term
of moral experience, and that truth, goodness, and
beauty are inevitably envisaged by any one whose
life has in some measure a rational quality. It is
of no religious interest in the sense that perhaps
some physical or dynamic absolute might be scientifically discoverable in the dark entrails of nature or of mind. The great difference between
religion and metaphysics is that religion looks for
God at the top of life and metaphysics at the bottom; a fact which explains why metaphysics has
such difficulty in finding God, while religion has
never lost him.

This brings us to the grand characteristic and
contradiction of Saint Augustine's philosophy, a
characteristic which can be best studied, perhaps,
in him, although it has been inherited by all Christian theology and was already present in Stoic and

Platonic speculation, when the latter had lost its ethical moorings. This is the idea that the same God who is the ideal of human aspiration is also the creator of the universe and its only primary substance.

If Plato, when he wrote that fine and profound passage in the sixth book of the Republic, where **Ambiguous** he says that the good is the cause of all **efficacy of** intelligence in the mind and of all in- **the good in** **Plato.** telligibility in the object, and indeed the principle of all essence and existence—if Plato could have foreseen what his oracular hyperbole was to breed in the world, we may well believe that he would have expunged it from his pages with the same severity with which he banished the poets from his State. In the lips of Socrates, and at that juncture in the argument of the Republic, those sentences have a legitimate meaning. The good is the principle of benefit, and the philosophers who are to rule the state will not be alienated by their contemplations from practical wisdom, seeing that the idea of the good—*i. e.,* of the advantageous, profitable, and beneficial—is the highest concept of the whole dialectic, that in reference to which all other ideas have place and significance. If we ventured to extend the interpretation of the passage, retaining its spirit, into fields where we have more knowledge than Plato could have, we might say that the principle of the good generates essence and existence, in the sense that all natural organs have functions and utilities by which they establish themselves in the world, and that the system of these useful functions is the true essence or idea of any living thing. But the Socratic origin and sense of such a passage as this, and of others (in the Timæus, for instance) allied to it, was soon lost in the headlong ideolatry which took possession of the neo-Platonic school; and it was through this medium that Saint Augustine received his Platonic inspiration. The good no longer meant, as it did to Plato, the principle of benefit everywhere, but it meant the good Being; and this, for a Christian, could naturally be none other than God; so that the idea that the good was the creator of all essence and existence now assumed a marvellously Mosaic significance. Here was one of those bits of primeval revelation which, it was explained, had survived in the heathen world. The hypostasis of moral conceptions, then, and of the idea of the good in particular, led up from the Platonic side to the doctrine of creation.

The history of the conception among the Jews was entirely different, the element of goodness in the creator being there adventitious and the element of power original. Jehovah for Job was a universal force, justified primarily by his omnipotence; but this physical authority would in the end, he hoped, be partly rationalised and made to clash less scandalously with the authority of justice. Among the Greeks, as was to be expected, the idea of justice

Ambiguous goodness of the creator in Job.

was more independent and entire; but once named
and enshrined, that divinity, too, tended to absoluteness, and could be confused with the physical
basis of existence. In the Stoic philosophy the
latter actually gained the upper hand, and the
problem of Job reappeared on the horizon. It did
not rise into painful prominence, however, until
Christian times, when absolute moral perfection
and absolute physical efficacy were predicated of
God with equal emphasis, if not among the people
who never have conceived God as either perfectly
good or entirely omnipotent, at least among the
theologians. If not all felt the contradiction with
equal acuteness, the reason doubtless was that a
large part of their thought was perfunctory and
merely apologetic: they did not quite mean what
they said when they spoke of perfect goodness;
and we shall see how Saint Augustine himself,
when reduced to extremities, surrendered his loyalty to the moral ideal rather than reconsider his
traditional premisses.

How tenaciously, however, he clung to the
moral in the religious, we can see by the difficulty
The   he had in separating himself from
Manicheans.   the Manicheans. The Manicheans admitted two absolutes, the essence of the one
being goodness and of the other badness. This
system was logically weak, because these absolutes were in the first place two, which is one
contradiction, and in the second place relative,
which is another. But in spite of the pitfalls

into which the Manicheans were betrayed by their pursuit of metaphysical absolutes, they were supported by a moral intuition of great truth and importance. They saw that an essentially good principle could not have essential evil for its effect. These moral terms are, we may ourselves feel sure, relative to existence and to actual impulse, and it may accordingly be always misleading to make them the essence of metaphysical realities: good and bad may be not existences but qualities which existences have only in relation to demands in themselves or in one another. Yet if we once launch, as many metaphysicians would have us do, into the hypostasis of qualities and relations, it is certainly better and more honest to make contradictory qualities into opposed entities, and not to render our metaphysical world unmeaning as well as fictitious by peopling it with concepts in which the most important categories of life are submerged and invalidated. Evil may be no more a metaphysical existence than good is; both are undoubtedly mere terms for vital utilities and impediments; but if we are to indulge in mythology at all, it is better that our mythology should do symbolic justice to experience and should represent by contrasted figures the ineradicable practical difference between the better and the worse, the beautiful and the ugly, the trustworthy and the fallacious. To discriminate between these things in practice is wisdom, and it should be the part of wisdom to discriminate between them in theory.

The Manicheans accordingly attributed what is good in the world to one power and what is bad to another. The fable is transparent enough, and we, who have only just learned to smile at a personal devil, may affect to wonder that any one should ever have taken it literally. But in an age when the assertive imagination was unchecked by any critical sense, such a device at least avoided the scandal of attributing all the evils and sins of this world to a principle essentially inviolate and pure. By avoiding what must have seemed a blasphemy to Saint Augustine, as to every one whose speculation was still relevant to his conscience and to his practical idealism, the Manicheans thus prevailed on many to overlook the contradictions which their system developed so soon as its figments were projected into the sphere of absolute existences.

The horror with which an idealistic youth at first views the truculence of nature and the turpitude of worldly life is capable of being softened by experience. Time subdues our initial preferences by showing us the complexity of moral relations in this world, and by extending our imaginative sympathy to forms of existence and passion at first repulsive, which from new and ultra-personal points of view may have their natural sweetness and value. In this way, Saint Augustine was ultimately brought to appreciate the catholicity and scope of those Greek sages who had taught that all being was to

All things good by nature.

itself good, that evil was but the impediment of
natural function, and that therefore the conception of anything totally or essentially evil was
only a petulance or exaggeration in moral judgment that took, as it were, the bit in its teeth,
and turned an incidental conflict of interests into
a metaphysical opposition of natures. All definite
being is in itself congruous with the true and the
good, since its constitution is intelligible and its
operation is creative of values. Were it not for
the limitations of matter and the accidental crowd-
ing and conflict of life, all existing natures might
subsist and prosper in peace and concord, just as
their various ideas live without contradiction in
the realm of conceptual truth. We may say of all
things, in the words of the Gospel, that their angels see the face of God. Their ideals are no less
cases of the good, no less instances of perfection,
than is the ideal locked in our private bosom. It
is the part of justice and charity to recognise this
situation, in view of which we may justly say that
evil is always relative and subordinate to some constituted nature in itself a standard of worth, a
point of departure for the moral valuation of
eventual changes and of surrounding things. Evil
is accordingly accidental and unnatural; it follows
upon the maladaptation of actions to natures and
of natures to one another. It can be no just
ground for the condemnation of any of those natural essences which only give rise to it by their
imperfect realisation.

The Semitic idea of creation could now receive
that philosophical interpretation which it so sadly
needed. Primordially, and in respect to what was
positive in them, all things might be expressions
of the good; in their essence and ideal state they
might be said to be created by God. For God was
the supreme ideal, to which all other goods were
subordinate and instrumental; and if we agree to
make a cosmogony out of morals and to hypostasise the series of rational ideals, taken in the in-
verse order, into a series of efficient causes, it is
clear that the highest good, which is at the end
of the moral scale, will now figure as a first cause
at the beginning of the physical sequence. This
operation is what is recorded and demanded in the
doctrine of creation: a doctrine which would lose
its dogmatic force if we allowed either the moral
ideality or the physical efficacy of the creator to
drop out of sight. If the moral ideality is sacrificed, we pass to an ordinary pantheism, while if
the physical efficacy is surrendered, we take refuge
in a naturalistic idealism of the Aristotelian type,
where the good is a function of things and neither
their substance nor their cause.

To accept the doctrine of creation, after it had
become familiar, was not very hard, because the
contradiction it contains could then be set down
to our imperfect apprehension. The unintelligibility of matters of fact does not lead us to deny
them, but merely to study them; and when the
creation was accepted as a fact, its unintelligibility

became merely a theological problem and a religious mystery, such as no mortal philosophy can be without. But for Saint Augustine the situation was wholly different. A doctrine of the creation had to be constructed: the disparate ideas had to be synthesised which posterity was afterward to regard as the obvious, if not wholly reconcilable, attributes of the deity. The mystery could not then be recognised; it had to be made. And Saint Augustine, with his vital religion, with his spontaneous adoration of God the ideal, could not attribute to that ideal unimpeded efficacy in the world. To admit that all natures were essentially good might dispel the Manichean fancy about an Evil Absolute engaged in single combat with an Absolute Good; but insight into the meaning and the natural conditions of evil could only make its presence more obvious and its origin more intimately bound up with the general constitution

The doctrine of the world. Evil is only imperfec-
of creation
demands that tion; but everything is imperfect. Con-
of the fall. flict is only maladaptation, but there is maladaptation everywhere. If we assume, then, what the doctrine of creation requires, that all things at first proceeded out of the potency of the good—their matter and form, their distribution and their energies, being wholly attributable to the attraction of the ultimately best—it is clear that some calamity must have immediately supervened by which the fountains of life were defiled, the strength of the ideal principle in living things

weakened, and the mortal conflict instituted which not only condemns all existent things ultimately to perish, but hardly allows them, even while they painfully endure, to be truly and adequately themselves.

Original sin, with the fall of the angels and of man for its mythical ground, thus enters into the inmost web of Augustinian philosophy. This fact cannot be too much insisted upon, for only by the immediate introduction of original sin into the history of the world could a man to whom God was still a moral term believe at all in the natural and fundamental efficacy of God in the cosmos. The doctrine of the fall made it possible for Saint Augustine to accept the doctrine of the creation. Both belonged to the same mythical region in which the moral values of life were made to figure as metaphysical agents; but when once the metaphysical agency of the highest good was admitted into a poetic cosmogony, it became imperative to admit also the metaphysical agency of sin into it; for otherwise the highest good would be deprived of its ideal and moral character, would cease to be the entelechy of rational life, and be degraded into a flat principle of description or synthesis for experience and nature as they actually are. God would thus become a natural agent, like the fire of Heraclitus, in which human piety could take an interest only by force of traditional inertia and unintelligence, while the continued muttering of the ritual prevented men from awaking to the dis-

appearance of the god. The essence of deity, as
Augustine was inwardly convinced, was correspon-
dence to human aspiration, moral perfection, and
ideality. God, therefore, as the Manicheans, with
Plato and Aristotle before them, had taught, could
be the author of good only; or, to express the same
thing in less figurative and misleading language,
it was only the good in things that could con-
tribute to our idea of divinity. What was evil
must, therefore, be carried up into another concept, must be referred, if you will, to another mythical agent; and this mythical agent in Saint Augustine's theology was named sin.

Everything in the world which obscured the image of the creator or rebelled against his com-
Original mandments (everything, that is, which
sin. prevented in things the expression of
their natural ideals) was due to sin. Sin was responsible for disease of mind and body, for all
suffering, for death, for ignorance, perversity, and
dulness. Sin was responsible—so truly *original*
was it—for what was painful and wrong even in
the animal kingdom, and sin—such was the paradoxical apex of this inverted series of causes—sin
was responsible for sin itself. The insoluble problems of the origin of evil and of freedom, in a
world produced in its every fibre by omnipotent
goodness, can never be understood until we remember their origin. They are artificial problems,
unknown to philosophy before it betook itself to
the literal justification of fables in which the ob-

jects of rational endeavour were represented as causes of natural existence. The former are internal products of life, the latter its external conditions. When the two are confused we reach the contradiction confronting Saint Augustine, and all who to this day have followed in his steps. The cause of everything must have been the cause of sin, yet the principle of good could not be the principle of evil. Both propositions were obviously true, and they were contradictory only after the mythical identification of the God which meant the ideal of life with the God which meant the forces of nature.

It would help us little, in trying to understand these doctrines, to work over the dialectic of them, **Forced** and seek to express the contradiction **abandonment** in somewhat veiled terms or according **of the ideal.** to new pictorial analogies. Good and evil, in the context of life, undoubtedly have common causes; but that system which involves both is for that very reason not an ideal system, and to represent it as such is simply to ignore the conscience and the upward effort of life. The contradiction can be avoided only by renouncing the meaning of one of the terms; either, that is, by no longer regarding the good as an absolute creator, but merely as a partial result or tendency in a living world whose life naturally involves values, or else by no longer conceiving God as the ideal term in man's own existence. The latter is the solution adopted by metaphysicians generally, and by Saint Augustine himself when hard pressed by the exigencies of his double allegiance. God, he tells us, is just, although not just as man is, *nor as man should be.* In other words, God is to be called just even when he is unjust in the only sense in which the word justice has a meaning among men. We are forced, in fact, to obscure our moral concepts and make them equivocal in order to be able to apply them to the efficient forces and actual habits of this world. The essence of divinity is no longer moral excellence, but ontological and dynamic relations to the natural world, so that the love of God would have to become, not an exercise of reason and conscience, as it naturally was with Saint Augustine, but a mystical intoxication, as it was with Spinoza.

The sad effects of this degradation of God into a physical power are not hard to trace in Augustine's own doctrine and feeling. He became a champion of arbitrary grace and arbitrary predestination to perdition. The eternal damnation of innocents gave him no qualms; and in this we must admire the strength of his logic, since if it is right that there should be wrong at all, there is no particular reason for stickling at the quantity or the enormity of it. And yet there are sentences which for their brutality and sycophancy cannot be read without pain—sentences inspired by this misguided desire to apologise for the crimes of the universe. " Why should God not create beings that he foreknew were to sin, when indeed in their persons and by their fates he could manifest both what punishment their guilt deserved and what free gifts he might bestow on them by his favour?" "Thinking it more lordly and better to do well even in the presence of evil than not to allow evil to exist at all." Here the pitiful maxim of doing evil that good may come is robbed of the excuse it finds in human limitations and is made the first principle of divine morality. Repellent and contorted as these ultimate metaphysical theories may seem, we must not suppose that they destroyed in Saint Augustine that practical and devotional idealism which they contradicted: the region of Christian charity is fortunately far wider and far nearer home than that of Christian apologetics. The work of practical redemption went on, while the dialectics about the perfection of the universe were forgotten; and Saint Augustine never ceased, by a happy inconsistency, to bewail the sins and to combat the heresies which his God was stealthily nursing, so that in their melodramatic punishment his glory might be more beautifully manifested.

It was Saint Augustine, as we know, who, in spite of his fervid Catholicism, was the favourite The problem master of both Luther and Calvin. among the They emphasised, however, his more Protestants. fanatical side, and this very predestinarian and absolutist doctrine which he had prevailed on himself to accept. Here was the pantheistic leaven doing its work; and concentration of attention on the Old Testament, given the reformers' controversial and metaphysical habit of thought, could only precipitate the inevitable. While popular piety bubbled up into all sorts of emotional and captious sects, each with its pathetic insistence on some text or on some whimsey, but all inwardly inspired by an earnest religious hunger, academic and cultivated Protestantism became every day more pale and rationalistic. Mediocre natures continued to rehearse the old platitudes and tread the slippery middle courses of one orthodoxy or another; but distinguished minds could no longer treat such survivals as more than allegories, historic or mythical illustrations of general spiritual truths. So Lessing, Goethe, and the idealists in Germany, and after them such lay prophets as Carlyle and Emerson, had for Christianity only an inessential respect. They drank their genuine inspiration directly from nature, from history, from the total personal apprehension they might have of life. In them speculative theology rediscovered its affinity to neo-Platonism; in other words, Christian philosophy was washed clean of its legendary alloy to become a pure cosmic speculation. It was Gnosticism come again in a very different age to men in an opposite phase of culture, but with its logic unchanged. The creation was the self-diremption of the infinite into finite expression, the fall was the self-discovery of this finitude, the incarnation was the awakening of the finite to its essential infinity; and here, a sufficient number of pages having been

engrossed, the matter generally hastened to a conclusion; for the redemption with its means of application, once the central point in Christianity,
was less pliable to the new pantheistic interpretation. Neo-Platonism had indeed cultivated asceticism, ecstasics, and a hope of reabsorption into the
One; but these things a modern, and especially a
Teutonic, temperament could hardly relish; and
though absolutism in a sense must discountenance
all finite interests and dissolve all experience, in
theory, into a neutral whole, yet this inevitable
mysticism remained, as with the Stoics, sternly optimistic, in order to respond to the vital social
forces which Protestantism embodied. The ethical
part of neo-Platonism and the corresponding
Christian doctrine of salvation had accordingly to
be discarded; for mystical as the northern soul
may gladly be in speculation, to satisfy its sentimentality, it hardly can be mystical in action, since
it has to satisfy also its interest in success and its
fidelity to instinct.

An absolutism which thus encourages and sanctions the natural will is Stoical and pantheistic;
it does not, like Indian and Platonic absolutism,
seek to suspend the will in view of some supernatural destiny. Pantheism subordinates morally what it finds to be dependent in existence;
its religion bids human reason and interest ab-
dicate before cosmic forces, instead of standing
out, like Buddhism and Christianity, for salvation,
for spiritual extrication, from a world which they

regard as delusive and fallen. The world of German absolutism, like the Stoic world, was not **Pantheism accepted.** fallen. On the contrary, it was divinely inspired and altogether authoritative; he alone who did not find his place and function in it was unholy and perverse. This world-worship, despising heartily every finite and rational ideal, gives to impulse and fact, whatever they may be, liberty to flourish under a divine warrant. Were the people accepting such a system corrupt, it would sanction their corruption, and thereby, most probably, lead to its own abandonment, for it would bring on an ascetic and supernaturalistic reaction by which its convenient sycophancy would be repudiated. But reflection and piety, even if their object be material and their worship idolatrous, exalt the mind and raise it above vulgar impulse. If you fetch from contemplation a theoretic license to be base, your contemplative habit itself will have purified you more than your doctrine will have power to degrade you afresh, for training affects instinct much more than opinion can. Antinomian theory can flourish blamelessly in a puritan soil, for there it instinctively remains theoretical. And the Teutonic pantheists are for the most part uncontaminated souls, puritan by training, and only interested in furthering the political and intellectual efficiency of the society in which they live. Their pantheism under these circumstances makes them the more energetic and turns them into prac-

tical positivists, docile to their social medium and
apologists for all its conventions. So that, while
they write books to disprove naturalism in natural
philosophy where it belongs, in morals where naturalism is treason they are themselves naturalists
of the most uncritical description, forgetting that
only the interests of the finite soul introduce such
a thing as good and evil into the world, and that
nature and society are so far from being authoritative and divine that they have no value whatever
save by the services they may render to each spirit
in its specific and genuine ambitions.

Indeed, this pantheistic subordination of conscience to what happens to exist, this optimism
Plainer scorn annulling every human ideal, betrays
for the ideal. its immoral tendency very clearly so
soon as it descends from theological seminaries
into the lay world. Poets at first begin to justify,
on its authority, their favourite passions and to
sing the picturesqueness of a blood-stained world.
" Practical " men follow, deprecating any reflection which may cast a doubt on the providential
justification of their chosen activities, and on the
invisible value of the same, however sordid, brutal,
or inane they may visibly be. Finally, politicians
learn to invoke destiny and the movement of the
age to save themselves the trouble of discerning
rational ends and to colour their secret indifference
to the world's happiness. The follies thus sanctioned theoretically, because they are involved in
a perfect world, would doubtless be perpetrated

none the less by the same persons had they absorbed in youth a different religion; for conduct is rooted in deep instincts which affect opinion more than opinion can avail to affect them in turn. Yet there is an added indignity in not preserving a clear and honest mind, and in quitting the world without having in some measure understood and appreciated it.

Pantheism is mythical and has, as we have just seen, all the subversive powers of ordinary super-

The price of mythology is superstition. stition. It turns the natural world, man's stamping-ground and system of opportunities, into a self-justifying and sacred life; it endows the blameless giant with an inhuman soul and then worships the monstrous divinity it has fabricated. It thereby encounters the same dilemma that defeats all mythology when it forgets its merely poetic office and trespasses upon moral ground. It must either interpret the natural world faithfully, attributing to the mythical deity the sort of life that dramatically suits its visible behaviour, or if it idealises and moralises the spectacle it must renounce the material reality and efficacy of its gods. Either the cosmic power must cover the actual goodness and badness in nature impartially, when to worship it would be idolatrous, or it must cover only the better side of nature, those aspects of it which support and resemble human virtue. In the latter case it is human virtue that mythology is formulating in a dramatic fiction, a human ideal that is being illustrated by a poet, who selects for the purpose certain phases of nature and experience. By this idealisation the affinity which things often have to man's interests may be brought out in a striking manner; but their total and real mechanism is no better represented than that of animals in Æsop's fables. To detect the divergence it suffices to open the eyes; and while nature may be rationally admired and cherished for so supporting the soul, it is her eventual ministry to man that makes her admirable, not her independent magnitude or antiquity. To worship nature as she really is, with all her innocent crimes made intentional by our mythology and her unfathomable constitution turned into a caricature of barbarian passions, is to subvert the order of values and to falsify natural philosophy. Yet this dislocation of reason, both in its conceptions and in its allegiance, is the natural outcome of thinking on mythical lines. A myth, by turning phenomena into expressions of thought and passion, teaches man to look for models and goals of action in that external world where reason can find nothing but instruments and materials.

CHAPTER X

PIETY

Hebraism is a striking example of a religion
tending to discard mythology and magic. It was
The core of religion not theoretical. a Hebraising apostle who said that
true religion and undefiled was to visit
the fatherless and the widow, and do
other works of mercy. Although a complete religion can hardly remain without theoretic and
ritual expression, we must remember that after all
religion has other aspects less conspicuous, perhaps,
than its mythology, but often more worthy of respect. If religion be, as we have assumed, an imaginative symbol for the Life of Reason, it should
contain not only symbolic ideas and rites, but also
symbolic sentiments and duties. And so it everywhere does in a notable fashion. Piety and spirituality are phases of religion no less important than
mythology, or than those metaphysical spectres
with which mythology terminates. It is therefore time we should quite explicitly turn from
religious ideas to religious emotions, from imaginative history and science to imaginative
morals.

Piety, in its nobler and Roman sense, may be said to mean man's reverent attachment to the sources of his being and the steadying of his life by that attachment. A soul is but the last bubble of a long fermentation in the world. If we wish to live associated with permanent racial interests we must plant ourselves on a broad historic and human foundation, we must absorb and interpret the past which has made us, so that we may hand down its heritage reinforced, if possible, and in no way undermined or denaturalised. This consciousness that the human spirit is derived and responsible, that all its functions are heritages and trusts, involves a sentiment of gratitude and duty which we may call piety.

The true objects of piety are, of course, those on which life and its interests really depend: parents first, then family, ancestors, and country; finally, humanity at large and the whole natural cosmos. But had a lay sentiment toward these forces been fostered by clear knowledge of their nature and relation to ourselves, the dutifulness or cosmic emotion thereby aroused would have remained purely moral and historical. As science would not in the end admit any myth which was not avowed poetry, so it would not admit any piety which was not plain reason and duty. But man, in his perplexities and pressing needs, has plunged, once for all, into imaginative courses through which it is our business to follow him, to see if he may not eventually reach

Loyalty to the sources of our being.

his goal even by those by-paths and dark circumlocutions.

What makes piety an integral part of traditional
religions is the fact that moral realities are rep-
The pious   resented in the popular mind by poetic
Æneas.   symbols. The awe inspired by principles so abstract and consequences so remote and
general is arrested at their conventional name.
We have all read in boyhood, perhaps with
derision, about the pious Æneas. His piety may
have seemed to us nothing but a feminine sensibility, a faculty of shedding tears on slight provo-
cation. But in truth Æneas's piety, as Virgil or
any Roman would have conceived it, lay less in
his feelings than in his function and vocation. He
was bearing the Palladium of his country to a new
land, to found another Troy, so that the blood and
traditions of his ancestors might not perish. His
emotions were only the appropriate expression of
his priestly office. The hero might have been stern
and stolid enough on his own martial ground, but
since he bore the old Anchises from the ruins of
Ilium he had assumed a sacred mission. Henceforth a sacerdotal unction and lyric pathos belonged rightfully to his person. If those embers,
so religiously guarded, should by chance have been
extinguished, there could never have been a Vestal
fire nor any Rome. So that all that Virgil and
his readers, if they had any piety, revered in the
world had been hazarded in those legendary adventures. It was not Æneas's own life or private

ambition that was at stake to justify his emotion.
His tenderness, like Virgil's own, was ennobled
and made heroic by its magnificent and impersonal
object. It was truly an epic destiny that inspired
both poet and hero.

If we look closer, however, we shall see that
mythical and magic elements were requisite to lend
An ideal   this loftiness to the argument. Had
background   Æneas not been Venus's son, had no
required.   prophetic instinct animated him, had
no Juno been planning the rise of Carthage, how
could the future destinies of this expedition have
been imported into it, to lift it above some pirat-
ical or desperate venture? Colonists passing in
our day to America or Australia might conceivably
carry with them the seeds of empires as considerable as Rome's. But they would go out thinking
of their private livelihood and convenience, break-
ing or loosening whatever pious bonds might unite
them to the past, and quite irresponsibly laying
the foundations for an unknown future. A poet,
to raise them to the height of their unwitting function, would have to endow them with second sight
and a corresponding breadth of soul and purpose.
He would need, in a word, heroic figures and supernatural machinery.

Now, what supernatural machinery and heroic
figures do for an epic poet piety does for a race.
It endows it, through mythical and magic symbols,
with something like a vision or representation of
its past and future. Religion is normally the most

traditional and national of things. It embodies
and localises the racial heritage. Commandments
of the law, feasts and fasts, temples and the tombs
associated with them, are so many foci of com-
munal life, so many points for the dissemination
of custom. The Sabbath, which a critical age
might justify on hygienic grounds, is inconceivable
without a religious sanction. The craving for rest
and emotion expressed itself spontaneously in a
practice which, as it established itself, had to be
sanctioned by fables till the recurrent holiday, with
all its humane and chastening influences, came to
be established on supernatural authority. It was
now piety to observe it and to commemorate in
it the sacred duties and traditions of the race. In
this function, of course, lay its true justification,
but the mythical one had to be assigned, since the
diffused prosaic advantages of such a practice would
never avail to impose it on irrational wills. Indeed, to revert to our illustration, had Æneas foreseen in detail the whole history of Rome, would
not his faith in his divine mission have been con-
siderably dashed? The reality, precious and in-
estimable as on the whole it was to humanity,
might well have shocked him by its cruelties,
shames, and disasters. He would have wished to
found only a perfect nation and a city eternal indeed. A want of rationality and measure in the
human will, that has not learned to prize small
betterments and finite but real goods, compels it
to deceive itself about the rewards of life in order

to secure them. That celestial mission, those heavenly apparitions, those incalculable treasures carried through many a storm, abused Æneas's mind in order to nerve him to his real duty. Yet his illusion was merely intellectual. The mission undertaken was truly worth carrying out. Piety thus came to bear the fruits of philanthropy in an age when the love of man was inconceivable. A dull and visionary intellect could hit on no other way of justifying a good instinct.

Philosophers who harbour illusions about the status of intellect in nature may feel that this leadership of instinct in moral life is a sort of indignity, and that to dwell on it so insistently is to prolong satire without wit. But the leadership of instinct, the conscious expression of mechanism, is not merely a necessity in the Life of Reason, it is a safeguard. Piety, in spite of its allegories, contains a much greater wisdom than a half-enlightened and pert intellect can attain. Natural beings have natural obligations, and the value of things for them is qualified by distance and by accidental material connections. Intellect would tend to gauge things impersonally by their intrinsic values, since intellect is itself a sort of disembodied and universal function; it would tend to disregard material conditions and that irrational substratum of reason without which reason would have no organs and no points of application. Piety,

on the contrary, esteems things apart from their
intrinsic worth, on account of their relation to the
Piety accepts agent's person and fortune. Yet such
natural con- esteem is perfectly rational, partiality
ditions and
present in man's affections and allegiance be-
tasks. ing justified by the partial nature and
local status of his life. Piety is the spirit's ac-
knowledgment of its incarnation. So, in filial and
parental affection, which is piety in an elementary
form, there is a moulding of will and emotion, a
check to irresponsible initiative, in obedience to
the facts of animal reproduction. Every living
creature has an intrinsic and ideal worth; he is
the centre of actual and yet more of potential interests. But this moral value, which even the re-
motest observer must recognise in both parent and
child, is not the ground of their specific affection
The for each other, which no other mortal
leadership of is called to feel in their regard. This
instinct is
normal. affection is based on the incidental and
irrational fact that the one has this particular man
for a father, and the other that particular man
for a son. Yet, considering the animal basis of
human life, an attachment resting on that circumstance is a necessary and rational attachment.

This physical bond should not, indeed, disturb
the intellect in its proper function or warp its judgments; you should not, under guise of tenderness,
become foolish and attribute to your father or
child greater stature or cleverness or goodness than
he actually possesses. To do so is a natural foible

but no part of piety or true loyalty. It is one
thing to lack a heart and another to possess eyes
and a just imagination. Indeed, piety is never
so beautiful and touching, never so thoroughly
humane and invincible, as when it is joined to an
impartial intellect, conscious of the relativity involved in existence and able to elude, through imaginative sympathy, the limits set to personal life
by circumstance and private duty. As a man dies
nobly when, awaiting his own extinction, he is interested to the last in what will continue to be the
interests and joys of others, so he is most profoundly pious who loves unreservedly a country,
friends, and associations which he knows very well
to be not the most beautiful on earth, and who,
being wholly content in his personal capacity with
his natural conditions, does not need to begrudge
other things whatever speculative admiration they
may truly deserve. The ideal in this polyglot
world, where reason can receive only local and temporal expression, is to understand all languages
and to speak but one, so as to unite, in a manly
fashion, comprehension with propriety.

Piety is in a sense pathetic because it involves
subordination to physical accident and acceptance
of finitude. But it is also noble and eminently
fruitful because, in subsuming a life under the
general laws of relativity, it meets fate with simple sincerity and labours in accordance with the
conditions imposed. Since man, though capable
of abstraction and impartiality, is rooted like a

vegetable to one point in space and time, and exists by limitation, piety belongs to the equilibrium of his being. It resides, so to speak, at his centre of gravity, at the heart and magnetic focus of his complex endowment. It exercises there the eminently sane function of calling thought home. It saves speculative and emotional life from hurtful extravagance by keeping it traditional and social. Conventional absurdities have at least this advantage, that they may be taken conventionally and may come to be, in practice, mere symbols for their uses. Piety is more closely linked with custom than with thought. It exercises an irrational suasion, moralises by contagion, and brings an emotional peace.

Patriotism is another form of piety in which its natural basis and rational function may be clearly

Embodiment essential to spirit.

seen. It is right to prefer our own country to all others, because we are children and citizens before we can be travellers or philosophers. Specific character is a necessary point of origin for universal relations: a pure nothing can have no radiation or scope. It is no accident for the soul to be embodied; her very essence is to express and bring to fruition the body's functions and resources. Its instincts make her ideals and its relations her world. A native country is a sort of second body, another enveloping organism to give the will definition. A specific inheritance strengthens the soul. Cosmopolitanism has doubtless its place, because a

man may well cultivate in himself, and represent
in his nation, affinities to other peoples, and such
assimilation to them as is compatible with personal
integrity and clearness of purpose. Plasticity to
things foreign need not be inconsistent with happiness and utility at home. But happiness and
utility are possible nowhere to a man who represents nothing and who looks out on the world
without a plot of his own to stand on, either on
earth or in heaven. He wanders from place to
place, a voluntary exile, always querulous, always
uneasy, always alone. His very criticisms express
no ideal. His experience is without sweetness,
without cumulative fruits, and his children, if he
has them, are without morality. For reason and
happiness are like other flowers—they wither when
plucked.

The object most commonly associated with piety
is the gods. Popular philosophy, inverting the
Piety to the natural order of ideas, thinks piety to
gods takes the gods the source of morality. But
form from
current piety, when genuine, is rather an in-
ideals. cidental expression of morality. Its
sources are perfectly natural. A volitional life that
reaches the level of reflection is necessarily moral
in proportion to the concreteness and harmony of
its instincts. The fruits which such harmonious
instincts, expressed in consciousness, may eventually bear, fruits which would be the aim of virtue,
are not readily imaginable, and the description of
them has long ago been intrusted to poets and

mythologists. Thus the love of God, for example,
is said to be the root of Christian charity, but is
in reality only its symbol. For no man not having
a superabundant need and faculty of loving real
things could have given a meaning to the phrase,
" love of God," or been moved by it to any action.
History shows in unequivocal fashion that the God
loved shifts his character with the shift in his
worshippers' real affections. What the psalmist
loves is the beauty of God's house and the place
where his glory dwelleth. A priestly quietude and
pride, a grateful, meditative leisure after the
storms of sedition and war, some retired unity of
mind after the contradictions of the world—this is
what the love of God might signify for the levites.
Saint John tells us that he who says he loves God
and loves not his neighbour is a liar. Here the
love of God is an anti-worldly estimation of things
and persons, a heart set on that kingdom of heaven
in which the humble and the meek should be exalted. Again, for modern Catholicism the phrase
has changed its meaning remarkably and signifies
in effect love for Christ's person, because piety
has taken a sentimental turn and centred on maintaining imaginary personal relations with the
Saviour. How should we conceive that a single
supernatural influence was actually responsible for
moral effects themselves so various, and producing,
in spite of a consecutive tradition, such various
notions concerning their object and supposed
source?

Mankind at large is also, to some minds, an object of piety. But this religion of humanity is

The religion of humanity.

rather a desideratum than a fact: humanity does not actually appear to anybody in a religious light. The *nihil homine homini utilius* remains a signal truth, but the collective influence of men and their average nature are far too mixed and ambiguous to fill the soul with veneration. Piety to mankind must be three-fourths pity. There are indeed specific human virtues, but they are those necessary to existence, like patience and courage. Supported on these indispensable habits, mankind always carries an indefinite load of misery and vice. Life spreads rankly in every wrong and impracticable direction as well as in profitable paths, and the slow and groping struggle with its own ignorance, inertia, and folly, leaves it covered in every age of history with filth and blood. It would hardly be possible to exaggerate man's wretchedness if it were not so easy to overestimate his sensibility. There is a *fond* of unhappiness in every bosom, but the depths are seldom probed; and there is no doubt that sometimes frivolity and sometimes sturdy habit helps to keep attention on the surface and to cover up the inner void. Certain moralists, without meaning to be satirical, often say that the sovereign cure for unhappiness is work. Unhappily, the work they recommend is better fitted to dull pain than to remove its cause. It occupies the faculties without rationalising the life. Before mankind could inspire even moderate satisfaction, not to speak of worship, its whole economy would have to be reformed, its reproduction regulated, its thoughts cleared up, its affections equalised and refined.

To worship mankind as it is would be to deprive it of what alone makes it akin to the divine— its aspiration. For this human dust lives; this misery and crime are dark in contrast to an imagined excellence; they are lighted up by a prospect of good. Man is not adorable, but he adores, and the object of his adoration may be discovered within him and elicited from his own soul. In this sense the religion of humanity is the only religion, all others being sparks and abstracts of the same. The indwelling ideal lends all the gods their divinity. No power, either physical or psychical, has the least moral prerogative nor any just place in religion at all unless it supports and advances the ideal native to the worshipper's soul. Without moral society between the votary and his god religion is pure idolatry; and even idolatry would be impossible but for the suspicion that somehow the brute force exorcised in prayer might help or mar some human undertaking.

There is, finally, a philosophic piety which has the universe for its object. This feeling, common Cosmic   to ancient and modern Stoics, has an piety.   obvious justification in man's dependence upon the natural world and in its service to many sides of the mind. Such justification of cosmic piety is rather obscured than supported by the euphemisms and ambiguities in which these philosophers usually indulge in their attempt to preserve the customary religious unction. For the more they personify the universe and give it the name of God the more they turn it into a devil. The universe, so far as we can observe it, is a wonderful and immense engine; its extent, its order, its beauty, its cruelty, makes it alike impressive. If we dramatise its life and conceive its spirit, we are filled with wonder, terror, and amusement, so magnificent is that spirit, so prolific, inexorable, grammatical, and dull. Like all animals and plants, the cosmos has its own way of doing things, not wholly rational nor ideally best, but patient, fatal, and fruitful. Great is this organism of mud and fire, terrible this vast, painful, glorious experiment. Why should we not look on the universe with piety? Is it not our substance? Are we made of other clay? All our possibilities lie from eternity hidden in its bosom. It is the dispenser of all our joys. We may address it without superstitious terrors; it is not wicked. It follows its own habits abstractedly; it can be trusted to be true to its word. Society is not impossible between it and us, and since it is the source of all our energies, the home of all our happiness, shall we not cling to it and praise it, seeing that it vegetates so grandly and so sadly, and that it is not for us to blame it for what, doubtless, it never knew that it did? Where there is such infinite

and laborious potency there is room for every hope.
If we should abstain from judging a father's errors
or a mother's foibles, why should we pronounce
sentence on the ignorant crimes of the universe,
which have passed into our own blood? The universe is the true Adam, the creation the true fall;
and as we have never blamed our mythical first
parent very much, in spite of the disproportionate
consequences of his sin, because we felt that he
was but human and that we, in his place, might
have sinned too, so we may easily forgive our real
ancestor, whose connatural sin we are from moment to moment committing, since it is only the
necessary rashness of venturing to be without fore-
knowing the price or the fruits of existence.

CHAPTER XI

SPIRITUALITY AND ITS CORRUPTIONS

In honouring the sources of life, piety is retrospective. It collects, as it were, food for morality,
To be spiritual is to live in view of the ideal. and fortifies it with natural and historic nutriment. But a digestive and formative principle must exist to assimilate this nutriment; a direction and an ideal have to be imposed on these gathered forces. So that religion has a second and a higher side, which looks to the end toward which we move as piety looks to the conditions of progress and to the sources from which we draw our energies. This aspiring side of religion may be called Spirituality. Spirituality is nobler than piety, because what would fulfil our being and make it worth having is what alone lends value to that being's source. Nothing can be lower or more wholly instrumental than the substance and cause of all things. The gift of existence would be worthless unless existence was good and supported at least a possible happiness. A man is spiritual when he lives in the presence of the ideal, and whether he eat or drink does so for the sake of a true and ultimate good. He is spiritual when he envisages his

193

goal so frankly that his whole material life becomes a transparent and transitive vehicle, an
instrument which scarcely arrests attention but
allows the spirit to use it economically and with
perfect detachment and freedom.

There is no need that this ideal should be pom-
pously or mystically described. A simple life is its
own reward, and continually realises its function.
Though a spiritual man may perfectly well go
through intricate processes of thought and attend
to very complex affairs, his single eye, fixed on a
rational purpose, will simplify morally the natural
chaos it looks upon and will remain free. This
spiritual mastery is, of course, no slashing and
forced synthesis of things into a system of philosophy which, even if it were thinkable, would leave
the conceived logical machine without ideality and
without responsiveness to actual interests; it is
rather an inward aim and fixity in affection that
knows what to take and what to leave in a world
over which it diffuses something of its own peace.
It threads its way through the landscape with so
little temptation to distraction that it can salute
every irrelevant thing, as Saint Francis did the
sun and moon, with courtesy and a certain affec-
tionate detachment.

Spirituality likes to say, Behold the lilies of the
field! For its secret has the same simplicity as
their vegetative art; only spirituality
has succeeded in adding consciousness
without confusing instinct. This success, unfor-

Spirituality natural.

tunately so rare in man's life as to seem paradoxical, is its whole achievement. Spirituality ought to have been a matter of course, since conscious existence has inherent value and there is no intrinsic ground why it should smother that value in alien ambitions and servitudes. But spirituality, though so natural and obvious a thing, is subject, like the lilies' beauty, to corruption. I know not what army of microbes evidently invaded from the beginning the soul's physical basis and devoured its tissues, so that sophistication and bad dreams entirely obscured her limpidity.

None the less, spirituality, or life in the ideal, must be regarded as the fundamental and native type of all life; what deviates from it is disease and incipient dissolution, and is itself what might plausibly demand explanation and evoke surprise. The spiritual man should be quite at home in a world made to be used; the firmament is spread over him like a tent for habitation, and sublunary furniture is even more obviously to be taken as a convenience. He cannot, indeed, remove mountains, but neither does he wish to do so. He comes to endow the mountains with a function, and takes them at that, as a painter might take his brushes and canvas. Their beauty, their metals, their pasturage, their defence—this is what he observes in them and celebrates in his addresses to them. The spiritual man, though not ashamed to be a beggar, is cognisant of what wealth can do and of what it cannot. His unworldliness is true

knowledge of the world, not so much a gaping
and busy acquaintance as a quiet comprehension
and estimation which, while it cannot come without intercourse, can very well lay intercourse aside.

If the essence of life be spiritual, early examples
of life would seem to be rather the opposite. But
Primitive man's view of primitive consciousness
consciousness is humanly biassed and relies too much
may be
spiritual. on partial analogies. We conceive an
animal's physical life in the gross, and must then
regard the momentary feelings that accompany it
as very poor expressions either of its extent or conditions. These feelings are, indeed, so many
ephemeral lives, containing no comprehensive view
of the animal's fortunes. They accordingly fail
to realise our notion of a spiritual human life which
would have to be rational and to form some representation of man's total environment and interests.
But it hardly follows that animal feelings are not
spiritual in their nature and, on their narrow
basis, perfectly ideal. The most ideal human passion is love, which is also the most absolute and
animal and one of the most ephemeral. Very
likely, if we could revert to an innocent and absorbed view of our early sensations, we should find
that each was a little spiritual universe like
Dante's, with its internal hell, purgatory, and
heaven. Cut off, as those experiences were, from
all vistas and from sympathy with things remote,
they would contain a closed circle of interests, a
flying glimpse of eternity. So an infant living

in his mystical limbo, without trailing in a literal sense any clouds of glory from elsewhere, might well repeat on a diminutive scale the beatific vision, insomuch as the only function of which he was conscious at all might be perfectly fulfilled by him and felt in its ideal import. Sucking and blinking are ridiculous processes, perhaps, but they may bring a thrill and satisfaction no less ideal than do the lark's inexhaustible palpitations. Narrow scope and low representative value are not defects in a consciousness having a narrow physical basis and comparatively simple conditions.

The spirit's foe in man has not been simplicity, but sophistication. His instincts, in becoming **Spirit crossed** many, became confused, and in grow-**by instru-** ing permanent, grew feeble and subject **mentalities.** to arrest and deviation. Nature, we may say, threw the brute form back into her cauldron, to smelt its substance again before pouring it into a rational mould. The docility which instinct, in its feebleness, acquired in the new creature was to be reason's opportunity, but before the larger harmony could be established a sorry chaos was bound to reign in the mind. Every peeping impulse would drop its dark hint and hide its head in confusion, while some pedantic and unjust law would be passed in its absence and without its vote. Secondary activities, which should always be representative, would establish themselves without being really such. Means would be pursued as if they were ends, and ends, under the illusion that they were forces, would be expected to further some activity, itself without justification. So pedantry might be substituted for wisdom, tyranny for government, superstition for morals, rhetoric for art.

This sophistication is what renders the pursuit of reason so perplexing and prolonged a problem. Half-formed adjustments in the brain and in the body politic are represented in consciousness by what are called passions, prejudices, motives, animosities. None of these felt ebullitions in the least understands its own causes, effects, or relations, but is hatched, so to speak, on the wing and flutters along in the direction of its momentary preference until it lapses, it knows not why, or is crossed and overwhelmed by some contrary power. Thus the vital elements, which in their comparative isolation in the lower animals might have yielded simple little dramas, each with its obvious ideal, its achievement, and its quietus, when mixed in the barbarous human will make a boisterous medley. For they are linked enough together to feel a strain, but not knit enough to form a harmony. In this way the unity of apperception seems to light up at first nothing but disunion. The first dawn of that rational principle which involves immortality breaks upon a discovery of death. The consequence is that ideality seems to man something supernatural and almost impossible. He finds himself at his awakening so confused that he puts chaos at the origin of the world. But only order can beget a world or evoke a sensation. Chaos is something secondary, composed of conflicting organisations interfering with one another. It is compounded like a common noise out of jumbled vibrations, each of which has its period and would in itself be musical. The problem is to arrange these sounds, naturally so tuneful, into concerted music. So long as total discord endures human life remains spasmodic and irresolute; it can find no ideal and admit no total representation of nature. Only when the disordered impulses and perceptions settle down into a trained instinct, a steady, vital response and adequate preparation for the world, do clear ideas and successful purposes arise in the mind. The Life of Reason, with all the arts, then begins its career.

The forces at play in this drama are, first, the primary impulses and functions represented by elementary values; second, the thin network of signals and responses by which those functions are woven into a total organ, represented by discursive thought and all secondary mental figments, and, third, the equilibrium and total power of that new organism in action represented by the ideal. Spirituality, which might have resided in the elementary values, sensuous or passionate, before the relational process supervened, can now exist only in the ultimate activity to which these processes are instrumental. Obstacles to spirituality in human life may accordingly take the form of an arrest either at the elementary values—an entanglement in sense and passion—or at the instrumental processes—an entanglement in what in religious parlance is called "the world."

Worldly minds bristle with conventional morality (though in private they may nurse a vice or two to appease wayward nature), and they are rational in everything except first principles. They consider the voluptuary a weak fool, disgraced and disreputable; and if they notice the spiritual man at all—for he is easily ignored—they regard him as a useless and visionary fellow. Civilisation has to work algebraically with symbols for known and unknown quantities which only in the end resume their concrete values, so that the journeymen and vulgar middlemen of the world know only conventional goods. They are lost in instrumentalities and are themselves only instruments in the Life of Reason. Wealth, station, fame, success of some notorious and outward sort, make their standard of happiness. Their chosen virtues are industry, good sense, probity, conventional piety, and whatever else has acknowledged utility and seemliness.

One foe of the spirit is worldliness.

In its strictures on pleasure and reverie this Philistia is perfectly right. Sensuous living (and I do not mean debauchery alone, but the palpitations of any poet without art or any mystic without discipline) is not only inconsequential and shallow, but dangerous to honour and to sincere happiness. When life remains lost in sense or reverts to it entirely, hu-

The case for and against pleasure.

manity itself is atrophied. And humanity is tormented and spoilt when, as more often happens, a man disbelieving in reason and out of humour with his world, abandons his soul to loose whimseys and passions that play a quarrelsome game there, like so many ill-bred children. Nevertheless, compared with the worldling's mental mechanism and rhetoric, the sensualist's soul is a well of wisdom. He lives naturally on an animal level and attains a kind of good. He has free and concrete pursuits, though they be momentary, and he has sincere satisfactions. He is less often corrupt than primitive, and even when corrupt he finds some justification for his captious existence. He harvests pleasures as he goes which intrinsically, as we have seen, may have the depth and ideality which nature breathes in all her oracles. His experience, for that reason, though disastrous is interesting and has some human pathos; it is easier to make a saint out of a libertine than out of a prig. True, the libertine is pursued, like the animals, by unforeseen tortures, decay, and abandonment, and he is vowed to a total death; but in these respects the worldly man has hardly an advantage. The Babels he piles up may indeed survive his person, but they are themselves vain and without issue, while his brief life has been meantime spent in slavery and his mind cramped with cant and foolish ambitions. The voluptuary is like some roving creature, browsing on nettles and living by chance; the worldling is like a beast of burden, now ill-used and over-

worked, now fatted, stalled, and richly caparisoned.
Æsop might well have described their relative
happiness in a fable about the wild ass and the
mule.

Thus, even if the voluptuary is sometimes a poet
and the worldling often an honest man, they both
lack reason so entirely that reflection revolts
equally against the life of both. Vanity, vanity,
is their common epitaph. Now, at the soul's chris-
tening and initiation into the Life of Reason, the
first vow must always be to " renounce the pomps
and vanities of this wicked world." A person to
whom this means nothing is one to whom, in the
end, nothing has meaning. He has not conceived
Upshot of a highest good, no ultimate goal is
worldly within his horizon, and it has never
wisdom. occurred to him to ask what he is living for. With all his pompous soberness, the
worldly man is fundamentally frivolous; with all
his maxims and cant estimations he is radically
inane. He conforms to religion without suspect-
ing what religion means, not being in the least
open to such an inquiry. He judges art like a
parrot, without having ever stopped to evoke an
image. He preaches about service and duty without any recognition of natural demands or any
standard of betterment. His moral life is one
vast anacoluthon in which the final term is left
out that might have given sense to the whole, one
vast ellipsis in which custom seems to bridge the
chasm left between ideas. He denies the values of

sense because they tempt to truancies from mechanical activity; the values of reason he necessarily ignores because they lie beyond his scope. He adheres to conventional maxims and material quantitative standards; his production is therefore, as far as he himself is concerned, an essential waste and his activity an essential tedium. If at least, like the sensualist, he enjoyed the process and expressed his fancy in his life, there would be something gained; and this sort of gain, though overlooked in the worldling's maxims, all of which have a categorical tone, is really what often lends his life some propriety and spirit. Business and war and any customary task may come to form, so to speak, an organ whose natural function will be just that operation, and the most abstract and secondary activity, like that of adding figures or reading advertisements, may in this way become the one function proper to some soul. There are Nibelungen dwelling by choice underground and happy pedants in the upper air.

Facts are not wanting for these pillars of society to take solace in, if they wish to defend their philosophy. The time will come, astronomers say, when life will be extinct upon this weary planet. All the delights of sense and imagination will be over. It is these that will have turned out to be vain. But the masses of matter which the worldlings have transformed with their machinery, and carried from one place to another, will remain to bear witness of them. The collocation of atoms

will never be what it would have been if their
feet had less continually beaten the earth. They
may have the proud happiness of knowing that,
when nothing that the spirit values endures, the
earth may still sometimes, because of them, cast a
slightly different shadow across the moon's craters.

There is no more critical moment in the life
of a man and a nation than that in which they
are first conscience-stricken and convicted of vanity. Failure, exhaustion,
confusion of aims, or whatever else it
be that causes a revulsion, brings them before a
serious dilemma. Has the vanity of life hitherto
been essential or incidental? Are we to look for
a new ambition, free from all the illusions of natural impulse, or are we rather to renounce all will
indiscriminately and fall back upon conformity
and consummate indifference? As this question
is answered in one way or the other, two different
types of unworldly religion arise.

The first, which heralds a new and unimpeach-
able special hope, a highest duty finally recognised
and driving out all lesser motives and
satisfactions from the soul, refers van-
ity to perversity, to error, to a sort of original misunderstanding of our own nature which has led
us, in pursuing our worldly interests, to pursue
in truth our own destruction. The vanity of life,
according to this belief, has been accidental. The
taint of existence is not innate vanity but casual
sin; what has misled us is not the will in general

but only the false and ignorant direction of a will not recognising its only possible satisfaction. What religion in this case opposes to the world is a special law, a special hope, a life intense, ambitious, and aggressive, but excluding much which to an ingenuous will might seem excellent and tempting. Worldliness, in a word, is here met by fanaticism.

The second type of unworldly religion does not propose to overwhelm the old Adam by single-
and mysticism. minded devotion to one selected interest, nor does it refer vanity to an accidental error. On the contrary, it conceives that any special interest, any claim made by a finite and mortal creature upon an infinite world, is bound to be defeated. It is not special acts, it conceives, which are sinful, but action and will themselves that are intrinsically foolish. The cure lies in rescinding the passionate interests that torment us, not in substituting for them another artificial passion more imperious and merciless than the natural passions it comes to devour. This form of religion accordingly meets worldliness with mysticism. Holiness is not placed in conformity to a prescriptive law, in pursuit of a slightly regenerated bliss, nor in advancing a special institution and doctrine. Holiness for the mystic consists rather in universal mildness and insight; in freedom from all passion, bias, and illusion; in a disembodied wisdom which accepts the world, dominates its labyrinths, and is able to guide others

through it, without pursuing, for its own part, any hope or desire.

If these two expedients of the conscience convicted of vanity were to be subjected to a critical **Both are** judgment, they would both be con-**irrational.** victed of vanity themselves. The case of fanaticism is not doubtful, for the choice it makes of a special law or institution or posthumous hope is purely arbitrary, and only to be justified by the satisfaction it affords to those very desires which it boasts to supplant. An oracular morality or revealed religion can hope to support its singular claims only by showing its general conformity to natural reason and its perfect beneficence in the world. Where such justification is wanting the system fanatically embraced is simply an epidemic mania, a social disease for the philosopher to study and, if possible, to cure. Every strong passion tends to dislodge the others, so that fanaticism may often involve a certain austerity, impetuosity, and intensity of life. This vigour, however, is seldom lasting; fanaticism dries its own roots and becomes, when traditionally established, a convention as arbitrary as any fashion and the nest for a new brood of mean and sinister habits. The Pharisee is a new worldling, only his little world is narrowed to a temple, a tribe, and a clerical tradition.

Mysticism, as its meditative nature comports, is never so pernicious, nor can it be brought so easily round to worldliness again. That its beneficent

element is purely natural and inconsistent with
a denial of will, we shall have occasion elsewhere
to observe. Suffice it here to point out, that even
if a moral nihilism could be carried through and
all definite interests abandoned, the vanity of life
would not be thereby corrected, but merely ex-
posed. When our steps had been retraced to the
very threshold of being, nothing better worth
doing would have been discovered on the way.
That to suffer illusion is a bad thing might ordinarily be taken for an axiom, because ordinarily
we assume that true knowledge and rational voli-
tion are possible; but if this assumption is denied,
the value of retracting illusions is itself impeached.
When vanity is represented as universal and salvation as purely negative, every one is left free
to declare that it is vain to renounce vanity and
sinful to seek salvation.

This result, fantastic though it may at first sight
appear, is one which mysticism actually comes to
under certain circumstances. Absolute pessimism
and absolute optimism are opposite sentiments attached to a doctrine identically the same. In
either case no improvement is possible, and the
authority of human ideals is denied. To escape,
to stanch natural wounds, to redeem society and
the private soul, are then mistaken and pitiable
ambitions, adding to their vanity a certain touch
of impiety. One who really believes that the
world's work is all providentially directed and that
whatever happens, no matter how calamitous or

shocking, happens by divine right, has a quietistic
excuse for license; to check energy by reason, and
seek to limit and choose its path, seems to him
a puny rebellion against omnipotence, which works
through madness and crime in man no less than
through cataclysms in outer nature. Every particular desire is vain and bound, perhaps, to be
defeated; but the mystic, when caught in the ex-
pansive mood, accepts this defeat itself as needful.
Thus a refusal to discriminate rationally or to accept human interests as the standard of right may
culminate in a convulsive surrender to passion, just
as, when caught in the contractile phase, the same
mysticism may lead to universal abstention.

Must unworldliness be either fanatical or mystical? That is a question of supreme importance
Is there a   to the moral philosopher. On the an-
third course? swer to it hangs the rationality of a
spiritual life; nay, the existence of spirituality
itself among the types of human activity. For the
fanatic and mystic are only spiritual in appearance because they separate themselves from the
prevalent interests of the world, the one by a special persistent aggression, the other by a general
passivity and unearthly calm. The fanatic is, not-
withstanding, nothing but a worldling too narrow
and violent to understand the world, while the
mystic is a sensualist too rapt and voluptuous to
rationalise his sensations. Both represent arrested
forms of common-sense, partial developments of
a perfectly usual sensibility. There is no divine

inspiration in having only one passion left, nor in dreamfully accepting or renouncing all the passions together. Spirituality, if identified with such types, might justly be called childish. There is an innocent and incredulous childishness, with its useless eyes wide open, just as there is a malevolent and peevish childishness, eaten up with some mischievous whim. The man of experience and affairs can very quickly form an opinion on such phenomena. He has no reason to expect superior wisdom in those quarters. On the contrary, his own customary political and humane stand-point gives him the only authoritative measure of their merits and possible uses. " These sectaries and dreamers," he will say to himself, " cannot understand one another nor the rôle they themselves play in society. It is for us to make the best of them we can, taking such prudent measures as are possible to enlist the forces they represent in works of common utility."

The philosopher's task, in these premisses, is to discover an escape from worldliness which shall

Yes; for experience has intrinsic inalienable values.

offer a rational advance over it, such as fanaticism and mysticism cannot afford. Does the Life of Reason differ from that of convention? Is there a spirituality really wiser than common-sense? That there is appears in many directions. Worldliness is arrest and absorption in the instrumentalities of life; but instrumentalities cannot exist without ultimate purposes, and it suffices to lift the eyes to those purposes and to question the will sincerely about its essential preferences, to institute a catalogue of rational goods, by pursuing any of which we escape worldliness. Sense itself is one of these goods. The sensualist at least is not worldly, and though his nature be atrophied in all its higher part, there is not lacking, as we have seen, a certain internal and abstract spirituality in his experience. He is a sort of sprightly and incidental mystic, treating his varied succession of little worlds as the mystic does his monotonous universe. Sense, moreover, is capable of many refinements, by which physical existence becomes its own reward. In the disciplined play of fancy which the fine arts afford, the mind's free action justifies itself and becomes intrinsically delightful. Science not only exercises in itself the intellectual powers, but assimilates nature to the mind, so that all things may nourish it. In love and friendship the liberal life extends also to the heart. All these interests, which justify themselves by their intrinsic fruits, make so many rational episodes and patches in conventional life; but it must be confessed in all candour that these are but oases in the desert, and that as the springs of life are irrational, so its most vehement and prevalent interests remain irrational to the end. When the pleasures of sense and art, of knowledge and sympathy, are stretched to the utmost, what part will they cover and justify of our passions, our industry, our governments, our religion?

It was a signal error in those rationalists who attributed their ideal retrospectively to nature that they grotesquely imagined that people were hungry so that they might enjoy eating, or curious in order to delight in discovering the truth, or in love the better to live in conscious harmony. Such a view forgets that all the forces of life work originally and fundamentally *a tergo,* that experience and reason are not the ground of preference but its result. In order to live men will work disproportionately and eat all manner of filth without pleasure; curiosity as often as not leads to illusion, and argument serves to foster hatred of the truth; finally, love is notoriously a great fountain of bitterness and frequently a prelude to crime and death. When we have skimmed from life its incidental successes, when we have harvested the moments in which existence justifies itself, its profound depths remain below in their obscure commotion, depths that breed indeed a rational efflorescence, but which are far from exhausted in producing it, and continually threaten, on the contrary, to engulf it.

The spiritual man needs, therefore, something more than a cultivated sympathy with the brighter scintillation of things. He needs to refer that scintillation to some essential light, so that in reviewing the motley aspects of experience he may not be reduced to culling superciliously the flowers that please him, but may view in them all

For these the religious imagination must supply an ideal standard.

only images and varied symbols of some eternal good. Spirituality has never flourished apart from religion, except momentarily, perhaps, in some master-mind, whose original intuitions at once became a religion to his followers. For it is religion that knows how to interpret the casual rationalities in the world and isolate their principle, setting this principle up in the face of nature as nature's standard and model. This ideal synthesis of all that is good, this consciousness that over earth floats its congenial heaven, this vision of perfection which gilds beauty and sanctifies grief, has taken form, for the most part, in such grossly material images, in a mythology so opaque and pseudo-physical, that its ideal and moral essence has been sadly obscured; nevertheless, every religion worthy of the name has put into its gods some element of real goodness, something by which they become representative of those scattered excellences and self-justifying bits of experience in which the Life of Reason consists.

That happy constitution which human life has at its best moments—that, says Aristotle, the divine life has continually. The philosopher thus expressed with absolute clearness the principle which the poets had been clumsily trying to embody from the beginning. Burdened as traditional faiths might be with cosmological and fanciful matter, they still presented in a conspicuous and permanent image that which made all good things good, the ideal and standard of all excellence. By the help of such symbols the spiritual man could steer and steady his judgment; he could say, according to the form religion had taken in his country, that the truly good was what God commanded, or what made man akin to the divine, or what led the soul to heaven. Such expressions, though taken more or less literally by a metaphysical intellect, did not wholly forfeit their practical and moral meaning. God, for a long time, was understood to command what in fact was truly important, the divine was long the truly noble and beautiful, heaven hardly ever ceased to respond to impersonal and ideal aspirations. Under those figures, therefore, the ideals of life could confront life with clearness and authority. The spiritual man, fixing his eyes on them, could live in the presence of ultimate purposes and ideal issues. Before each immediate task, each incidental pleasure, each casual success, he could retain his sweetness and constancy, accepting what good these moments brought and laying it on the altar of what they ought to bring.

CHAPTER XII

CHARITY

Those whom a genuine spirituality has freed from the foolish enchantment of words and con-

Possible tyranny of reason. ventions and brought back to a natural ideal, have still another illusion to vanquish, one into which the very concentration and deepening of their life might lead them. This illusion is that they and their chosen interests alone are important or have a legitimate place in the moral world. Having discovered what is really good for themselves, they assume that the like is good for everybody. Having made a tolerable synthesis and purification of their own natures, they require every other nature to be composed of the same elements similarly combined. What they have vanquished in themselves they disregard in others; and the consequence sometimes is that an impossibly simplified and inconsiderate regimen is proposed to mankind, altogether unrepresentative of their total interests. Spiritual men, in a word, may fall into the aristocrat's fallacy; they may forget the infinite animal and vulgar life which remains

214

quite disjointed, impulsive, and short-winded, but which nevertheless palpitates with joys and sorrows, and makes after all the bulk of moral values in this democratic world.

After adopting an ideal it is necessary, therefore, without abandoning it, to recognise its rela-
Everything tivity. The right path is in such a
has its rights. matter rather difficult to keep to. On the one hand lies fanatical insistence on an ideal once arrived at, no matter how many instincts and interests (the basis of all ideals) are thereby outraged in others and ultimately also in one's self. On the other hand lies mystical disintegration, which leads men to feel so keenly the rights of everything in particular and of the All in general, that they retain no hearty allegiance to any human interest. Between these two abysses winds the narrow path of charity and valour. The ultimate ideal is absolutely authoritative, because if any ground were found to relax allegiance to it in any degree or for any consideration, that ground would itself be the ideal, found to be more nearly absolute and ultimate than the one, hastily so called, which it corrected. The ultimate ideal, in order to maintain its finality and preclude the possibility of an appeal which should dislodge it from its place of authority, must have taken all interests into consideration; it must be universally representative. Now, to take an interest into consideration and represent it means to intend, as far as possible, to

secure the particular good which that particular interest looks to, and never, whatever measures may be adopted, to cease to look back on the elementary impulse as upon something which ought, if possible, to have been satisfied, and which we should still go back and satisfy now, if circumstances and the claims of rival interests permitted.

Justice and charity are identical. To deny the initial right of any impulse is not morality but fanaticism. However determined may be the prohibition which reason opposes to some wild instinct, that prohibition is never reckless; it is never inconsiderate of the very impulse which it suppresses. It suppresses that impulse unwillingly, pitifully, under stress of compulsion and *force majeure;* for reason, in representing this impulse in the context of life and in relation to every other impulse which, in its operation, it would affect mechanically, rejects and condemns it; but it condemns it not by antecedent hate but by supervening wisdom. The texture of the natural world, the conflict of interests in the soul and in society, all of which cannot be satisfied together, is accordingly the ground for moral restrictions and compromises. Whatever the upshot of the struggle may be, whatever the verdict pronounced by reason, the parties to the suit must in justice all be heard, and heard sympathetically.

Herein lies the great difference between first-hand and second-hand morality. The retailers of moral truth, the town-criers that go shouting in the streets some sentence passed long ago in **Primary and** reason's court against some inadmis-**secondary** sible desire, know nothing of justice **morality.** or mercy or reason—three principles essentially identical. They thunder conclusions without remembering the premises, and expose their precepts, daily, of course, grown more thin and unrepresentative, to the aversion and neglect of all who genuinely love what is good. The masters of life, on the contrary, the first framers and discoverers of moral ideals, are persons who disregard those worn conventions and their professional interpreters: they are persons who have a fresh sense for the universal need and cry of human souls, and reconstruct the world of duty to make it fit better with the world of desire and of possible happiness. Primary morality, inspired by love of something naturally good, is accordingly charitable and ready to forgive; while secondary morality, founded on prejudice, is fanatical and ruthless.

As virtue carries with it a pleasure which perfects it and without which virtue would evidently **Uncharitable** be spurious and merely compulsory, so **pagan justice** justice carries with it a charity which **is not just.** is its highest expression, without which justice remains only an organised wrong. Of justice without charity we have a classic illustration in Plato's Republic and in general in the pagan world. An end is assumed, in this case

an end which involves radical injustice toward
every interest not included in it; and then an
organism is developed or conceived that shall sub-
serve that end, and political justice is defined as
the harmonious adjustment of powers and functions within that organism. Reason and art suffice to discover the right methods for reaching
the chosen end, and the polity thus established,
with all its severities and sacrifices of personal
will, is rationally grounded. The chosen end,
however, is arbitrary, and, in fact, perverse; for
to maintain a conventional city with stable institutions and perpetual military efficiency would
not secure human happiness; nor (to pass to the
individual virtue symbolised by such a state)
would the corresponding discipline of personal
habits, in the service of vested interests and bodily
life, truly unfold the potentialities of the human
spirit.

Plato himself, in passing, acknowledges that
his political ideal is secondary and not ideal
at all, since only luxury, corruption, and physical
accidents make a military state necessary; but
his absorption in current Greek questions made
him neglect the initial question of all, namely,
how a non-military and non-competitive state
might be established, or rather how the remedial
functions of the state might be forestalled by
natural justice and rendered unnecessary. The
violence which such a fallen ideal, with its in-
iquitous virtues, does to humanity appeared only

too clearly in the sequel, when Platonism took refuge in the supernatural. The whole pagan world was convicted of injustice and the cities for whose glory the greatest heroes had lived and died were abandoned with horror. Only in a catacomb or a hermitage did there seem to be any room for the soul. This revulsion, perverse in its own way, expressed rightly enough the perversity of that unjust justice, those worldly and arbitrary virtues, and that sad happiness which had enslaved the world.

Plato could never have answered the question whether his Republic had a right to exist and to brush aside all other commonwealths; **The doom of ancient republics.** he could never have justified the ways of man to the rest of creation nor (what is more pertinent) to man's more plastic and tenderer imagination. The initial impulses on which his Republic is founded, which make war, defensive and aggressive, the first business of the state, are not irresistible impulses, they do not correspond to ultimate ends. Physical life cannot justify itself; it cannot be made the purpose of those rational faculties which it generates; these, on the contrary, are its own end. The purpose of war must be peace; the purpose of competition a more general prosperity; the purpose of personal life ideal achievements. A polity which should not tend to abolish private lusts, competition, and war would be an irrational polity. The organisation which the ancients insisted on within each state, the sacrifices they imposed on each class in the community for the general welfare, have to be repeated in that greater commonwealth of which cities and nations are citizens; for their own existence and prosperity depends on conciliating inwardly all that may affect them and turning foreign forces, when contact with them is inevitable, into friends. Duty and co-operation must extend as far as do physical bonds, the function of reason being to bring life into harmony with its conditions, so as to render it self-perpetuating and free. This end can never be attained while the scope of moral fellowship is narrower than that of physical interplay. Ancient civilisation, brilliant in proportion to its inner integration, was brief in proportion to its outer injustice. By defying the external forces on which also a commonwealth depends, those commonwealths came to premature extinction.

There is accordingly a justice deeper and milder than that of pagan states, a universal justice called charity, a kind of all-penetrating courtesy, by which the limits of personal or corporate interests are transgressed in imagination. Value is attributed to rival forms of life; something of the intensity and narrowness inherent in the private will is surrendered to admiration and solicitude for what is most alien and hostile to one's self. When this imaginative expansion ends in neutralising the will altogether, we have mysticism; but when it

Rational charity.

serves merely to co-ordinate felt interests with
other actual interests conceived sympathetically,
and to make them converge, we have justice and
charity.   Charity is nothing but a radical and
imaginative justice.   So the Buddhist stretches
his sympathy to all real beings and to many imaginary monsters; so the Christian chooses for
his love the diseased, the sinful, the unlovely.
His own salvation does not seem to either complete unless every other creature also is redeemed
and forgiven.

Such universal solicitude is rational, however,
only when the beings to which it extends are in
Its limits.   practical efficient relations with the
life that would co-operate with theirs.   In other
words, charity extends only to physical and discoverable creatures, whose destiny is interwoven
dynamically with our own.   Absolute and irresponsible fancy can be the basis of no duty.   If
not to take other real forces and interests into
account made classic states unstable and unjust,
to take into consideration purely imaginary forces
yields a polity founded on superstition, one unjust to those who live under it.   A compromise
made with non-existent or irrelevant interests is a
wrong to the real interests on which that sacrifice
is imposed gratuitously.   All sacrifices exacted
by mere religion have accordingly been inhuman;
at best they have unintentionally made some
amends by affording abstract discipline or artistic forms of expression.   The sacrifice must be

fruitful in the end and bring happiness to somebody: otherwise it cannot long remain tender or beautiful.

Charity is seldom found uncoloured by fables which illustrate it and lend it a motive by which Its mythical it can justify itself verbally. Metemsupports. psychosis, heaven and hell, Christ's suffering for every sinner, are notions by which charity has often been guided and warmed. Like myth everywhere, these notions express judgments which they do not originate, although they may strengthen or distort them in giving them expression. The same myths, in cruel hands, become goads to fanaticism. That natural sensitiveness in which charity consists has many degrees and many inequalities; the spirit bloweth where it listeth. Incidental circumstances determine its phases and attachments in life. Christian charity, for instance, has two chief parts: first, it hastens to relieve the body; then, forgetting physical economy altogether, it proceeds to redeem the soul. The bodily works of mercy which Christians perform with so much tact and devotion are not such as philanthropy alone would inspire; they are more and less than that. They are more, because they are done with a certain disproportionate and absolute solicitude, quite apart from ultimate benefit or a thought of the best distribution of energies; they are also less, because they stop at healing, and cannot pass beyond the remedial and incidental phase

without ceasing to be Christian. The poor, says
Christian charity, we have always with us; every
man must be a sinner—else what obligation
should he have to repent?—and, in fine, this
world is essentially the kingdom of Satan. Charity comes only to relieve the most urgent bodily
needs, and then to wean the heart altogether
from mortal interests. Thus Christianity covers
the world with hospitals and orphanages; but
its only positive labours go on in churches and
convents, nor will it found schools, if left to itself,
to teach anything except religion. These offices
may be performed with more or less success, with
more or less appeal to the miraculous; but, with
whatever mixture of magic and policy, Christian
charity has never aimed at anything but healing
the body and saving the soul.

Christ himself, we may well feel, did not affect
publicans and sinners, ignorant people and children, in order to save them in the
There is intelligence in charity. regimental and prescriptive fashion
adopted by the Church. He com-
manded those he forgave to sin no more and those
he healed to go, as custom would have it, to the
priest. He understood the bright good that each
sinner was following when he stumbled into the
pit. For this insight he was loved. To be re-
buked in that sympathetic spirit was to be com-
forted; to be punished by such a hand was to be
made whole. The Magdalene was forgiven because she had loved much; an absolution which

rehabilitates the primary longing that had driven
her on, a longing not insulted but comprehended
in such an absolution, and purified by that comprehension. It is a charitable salvation which
enables the newly revealed deity to be absolutely
loved. Charity has this art of making men abandon their errors without asking them to forget
their ideals.

In Buddhism the same charity wears a more
speculative form. All beings are to be redeemed

**Buddhist and
Christian
forms of it.**
from the illusion which is the fountain of their troubles. None is to be
compelled to assume irrationally an
alien set of duties or other functions than his
own. Spirit is not to be incarcerated perpetually
in grotesque and accidental monsters, but to be
freed from all fatality and compulsion. The goal
is not some more flattering incarnation, but escape from incarnation altogether. Ignorance is
to be enlightened, passion calmed, mistaken destiny revoked; only what the inmost being desid-
erates, only what can really quiet the longings
embodied in any particular will, is to occupy the
redeemed mind. Here, though creative reason is
wholly wanting, charity is truly understood; for
it avails little to make of kindness a vicarious
selfishness and to use neighbourly offices to
plunge our neighbour deeper into his favourite
follies. Such servile sympathy would make men
one another's accomplices rather than friends.
It would treat them with a weak promiscuous

favour, not with true mercy and justice. In charity there can be nothing to repent of, as there so often is in natural love and in partisan propaganda. Christians have sometimes interpreted charity as zeal to bring men into their particular fold; or, at other times, when enthusiasm for doctrine and institutes has cooled, they have interpreted charity to be mere blind co-operation, no matter in what.

The Buddhists seem to have shown a finer sense in their ministry, knowing how to combine universal sympathy with perfect spirituality. There was no brow-beating in their call to conversion, no new tyranny imposed of sanctioned by their promised deliverance. If they could not rise to a positive conception of natural life, this inability but marks the well-known limitations of Oriental fancy, which has never been able to distinguish steadily that imagination which rests on and expresses material life from that which, in its import, breaks loose from the given conditions of life altogether, and is therefore monstrous and dreamful. But at least Buddhism knew how to sound the heart and pierce to the genuine principles of happiness and misery. If it did not venture to interpret reason positively, it at least forbore to usurp its inward and autonomous authority, and did not set up, in the name of salvation, some new partiality, some new principle of distress and illusion. In destroying worldliness this religion avoided imposture. The

clearing it made in the soul was soon overgrown
again by the inexorable Indian jungle; but had
a virile intellect been at hand, it would have been
free to raise something solid and rational in the
space so happily swept clean of all accumulated
rubbish.

Against avarice, lust, and rancour, against
cruel and vain national ambitions, tenderer and
Apparent more recollected minds have always
division of sought some asylum; but they have
the spiritual
and the seldom possessed enough knowledge
natural. of nature and of human life to distinguish clearly the genuine and innocent goods
which they longed for, and their protest against
" the world " has too often taken on a mystical
and irrational accent. Charity, for instance, in
its profounder deliverances, has become a protest
against the illusion of personality; whereby existence and action seem to be wholly condemned
after their principle has been identified with selfishness. An artificial puzzle is thus created, the
same concept, selfishness or an irrational partiality and injustice in the will, being applied to two
principles of action, the one wrong and the other
necessary. Every man is necessarily the seat of
his own desires, which, if truly fulfilled, would
bring him satisfaction; but the objects in which
that satisfaction may be found, and the forces
that must co-operate to secure it, lie far afield,
and his life will remain cramped and self-
destructive so long as he does not envisage its

whole basis and co-operate with all his potential allies.

The rationality which would then be attained is so immensely exalted above the microscopic vision and punctiform sensibility of those who think themselves practical, that speculative natures seem to be proclaiming another set of interests, another and quite miraculous life, when they attempt to thaw out and vivify the vulgar mechanism; and the sense of estrangement and contradiction often comes over the spiritually minded themselves, making them confess sadly that the kingdom of heaven is not of this world. As common morality itself falls easily into mythical expressions and speaks of a fight between conscience and nature, reason and the passions, as if these were independent in their origin or could be divided in their operation, so spiritual life even more readily opposes the ideal to the real, the revealed and heavenly truth to the extant reality, as if the one could be anything but an expression and fulfilment of the other. Being equal convinced that spiritual life is authoritative and possible, and that it is opposed to all that earthly experience has as yet supplied, the prophet almost inevitably speaks of another world above the clouds and another existence beyond the grave; he thus seeks to clothe in concrete and imaginable form the ideal to which natural existence seems to him wholly rebellious. Spiritual life comes to mean life abstracted from politics, from art, from sense, even in the end from morality. Natural motives and natural virtues are contrasted with those which are henceforth called supernatural, and all the grounds and sanctions of right living are transferred to another life. A doctrine of immortality thus becomes the favourite expression of religion. By its variations and greater or less transparency and ideality we can measure the degree of spiritual insight which has been reached at any moment.

CHAPTER XIII

THE BELIEF IN A FUTURE LIFE

At no point are the two ingredients of religion, superstition and moral truth, more often confused **The length** than in the doctrine of immortality, **of life a sub-** yet in none are they more clearly dis- **ject for** **natural** tinguishable. Ideal immortality is a **science.** principle revealed to insight; it is seen by observing the eternal quality of ideas and validities, and the affinity to them native to reason or the cognitive energy of mind. A future life, on the contrary, is a matter for faith or presumption; it is a prophetic hypothesis regarding occult existences. This latter question is scientific and empirical, and should be treated as such. A man is, forensically speaking, the same man after the nightly break in his consciousness. After many changes in his body and after long oblivion, parcels of his youth may be revived and may come to figure again among the factors in his action. Similarly, if evidence to that effect were available, we might establish the resurrection of a given soul in new bodies or its activity in remote places and times. Evidence

229

of this sort has in fact always been offered copi-
ously by rumour and superstition. The operation of departed spirits, like that of the gods,
has been recognised in many a dream, or message,
or opportune succour. The Dioscuri and Saint
James the Apostle have appeared—preferably on
white horses—in sundry battles. Spirits duly invoked have repeated forgotten gossip and revealed
the places where crimes had been committed or
treasure buried. More often, perhaps, ghosts
have walked the night without any ostensible or
useful purpose, apparently in obedience to some
ghastly compulsion that crept over them in death,
as if a hesitating sickle had left them still hanging to life by one attenuated fibre.

The mass of this evidence, ancient and modern,
traditional and statistical, is beneath considera-
"Psychical"   tion; the palpitating mood in which it
phenomena.   is gathered and received, even when
ostensibly scientific, is such that gullibility and
fiction play a very large part in the report; for it
is not to be assumed that a man, because he speaks
in the first person and addresses a learned society,
has lost the primordial faculty of lying. When
due allowance has been made, however, for legend
and fraud, there remains a certain residuum of
clairvoyance and telepathy, and an occasional
abnormal obedience of matter to mind which
might pass for magic. There are unmistakable
indications that in these regions we touch lower
and more rudimentary faculties. There seems to

be, as is quite natural, a sub-human sensibility in man, wherein ideas are connected together by bonds so irrational and tenacious that they seem miraculous to a mind already trained in practical and relevant thinking. This sub-human sense, far from representing important truths more clearly than ordinary apprehension can, reduces consciousness again to a tangle of trivial impressions, shots of uncertain range, as if a skin had not yet formed over the body. It emerges in tense and disorganised moments. Its reports are the more trifling the more startingly literal their veracity. It seems to represent a stratum of life beneath moral or intellectual functions, and beneath all personality. When proof has been found that a ghost has actually been seen, proof is required that the phantom has been rightly recognised and named; and this imputed identity is never demonstrable and in most cases impossible. So in the magic cures which from time immemorial have been recorded at shrines of all religions, and which have been attributed to wonder-workers of every sect: the one thing certain about them is that they prove neither the truth of whatever myth is capriciously associated with them, nor the goodness or voluntary power of the miracle-worker himself. Healer and medium are alike vehicles for some elemental energy they cannot control, and which as often as not misses fire; at best they feel a power going out of them which they themselves undergo, and which radiates from them like electricity, to work, as chance will have it, good or evil in the world. The whole operation lies, in so far as it really takes place at all, on the lowest levels of unintelligence, in a region closely allied to madness in consciousness and to sporadic organic impulses in the physical sphere.

Among the blind, the retina having lost its function, the rest of the skin is said to recover Hypertrophies its primordial sensitiveness to dis-of sense. tance and light, so that the sightless have a clearer premonition of objects about them than seeing people could have in the dark. So when reason and the ordinary processes of sense are in abeyance a certain universal sensibility seems to return to the soul; influences at other times not appreciable make then a sensible impression, and automatic reactions may be run through in response to a stimulus normally quite insufficient. Now the complexity of nature is prodigious; everything that happens leaves, like buried cities, almost indelible traces which an eye, by chance attentive and duly prepared, can manage to read, recovering for a moment the image of an extinct life. Symbols, illegible to reason, can thus sometimes read themselves out in trance and madness. Faint vestiges may be found in matter of forms which it once wore, or which, like a perfume, impregnated and got lodgment within it. Slight echoes may suddenly reconstitute themselves in the mind's silence; and a half-

stunned consciousness may catch brief glimpses of
long-lost and irrelevant things. Real ghosts are
such reverberations of the past, exceeding ordinary imagination and discernment both in vivid-
ness and in fidelity; they may not be explicable
without appealing to material influences subtler
than those ordinarily recognised, as they are
obviously not discoverable without some derange-
ment and hypertrophy of the senses.

That such subtler influences should exist is
entirely consonant with reason and experience;
These possi- but only a hankering tenderness for
bilities affect superstition, a failure to appreciate
physical
existence the function both of religion and of
only. science, can lead to reverence for
such oracular gibberish as these influences pro-
voke. The world is weary of experimenting
with magic. In utter seriousness and with immense solemnity whole races have given themselves up to exploiting these shabby mysteries;
and while a new survey of the facts, in the light
of natural science and psychology, is certainly not
superfluous, it can be expected to lead to nothing
but a more detailed and conscientious description
of natural processes. The thought of employing
such investigations to save at the last moment
religious doctrines founded on moral ideas is a
pathetic blunder; the obscene supernatural has
nothing to do with rational religion. If it were
discovered that wretched echoes of a past life
could be actually heard by putting one's ear long

enough to a tomb, and if (*per impossibile*) those
echoes could be legitimately attributed to another
mind, and to the very mind, indeed, whose former
body was interred there, a melancholy chapter
would indeed be added to man's earthly fortunes,
since it would appear that even after death he
retained, under certain conditions, a fatal attachment to his dead body and to the other material
instruments of his earthly life. Obviously such
a discovery would teach us more about dying
than about immortality; the truths disclosed,
since they would be disclosed by experiment and
observation, would be psycho-physical truths, im-
plying nothing about what a truly disembodied
life might be, if one were attainable; for a disembodied life could by no possibility betray itself
in spectres, rumblings, and spasms. Actual thun-
ders from Sinai and an actual discovery of two
stone tables would have been utterly irrelevant to
the moral authority of the ten commandments or
to the existence of a truly supreme being. No
less irrelevant to a supramundane immortality
is the length of time during which human spirits
may be condemned to operate on earth after their
bodies are quiet. In other words, spectral survivals would at most enlarge our conception of
the soul's physical basis, spreading out the area
of its manifestations; they could not possibly, seeing the survivals are physical, reveal the disembodied existence of the soul.

Such a disembodied existence, removed by its

nature from the sphere of empirical evidence,

Moral grounds for the doctrine. The necessary assumption of a future. might nevertheless be actual, and grounds of a moral or metaphysical type might be sought for postulating its reality. Life and the will to live are at bottom identical. Experience itself is transitive and can hardly arise apart from a forward effort and prophetic apprehension by which adjustments are made to a future unmistakably foreseen. This premonition, by which action seeks to justify and explain itself to reflection, may be analysed into a group of memories and sensations of movement, generating ideal expectations which might easily be disappointed; but scepticism about the future can hardly be maintained in the heat of action. A postulate acted on is an act of genuine and dogmatic faith. I not only postulate a morrow when I prepare for it, but ingenuously and heartily believe that the morrow will come. This faith does not amount to certitude; I may confess, if challenged, that before to-morrow I and the world and time itself might conceivably come to an end together; but that idle possibility, so long as it does not slacken action, will not disturb belief. Every moment of life accordingly trusts that life will continue; and this prophetic interpretation of action, so long as action lasts, amounts to continual faith in futurity.

A sophist might easily transform this psychological necessity into a dazzling proof of immortality. To believe anything, he might say, is to be active; but action involves faith in a future

An assumption no evidence. and in the fruits of action; and as no living moment can be without this confidence, belief in extinction would be self-contradictory and at no moment a possible belief. The question, however, is not whether every given moment has or has not a specious future before it to which it looks forward, but whether the realisation of such foresight, a realisation which during waking life is roughly usual, is incapable of failing. Now expectation, never without its requisite antecedents and natural necessity, often lacks fulfilment, and never finds its fulfilment entire; so that the necessity of a postulate gives no warrant for its verification. Expectation and action are constantly suspended together; and what happens whenever thought loses itself or stumbles, what happens whenever in its shifts it forgets its former objects, might well happen at crucial times to that train of intentions which we call a particular life or the life of humanity. The prophecy involved in action is not insignificant, but it is notoriously fallible and depends for its fulfilment on external conditions. The question accordingly really is whether a man expecting to live for ever or one expecting to die in his time has the more representative and trustworthy notion of the future. The question, so stated, cannot be solved by an appeal to evidence, which is necessarily all on one side, but only by criticising the value of evidence as against instinct and hope, and by ascertaining the relative status which assumption and observation have in experience.

The transcendental compulsion under which action labours of envisaging a future, and the animal instinct that clings to life and flees from death as the most dreadful of evils are the real grounds why immortality seems initially natural and good. Confidence in living for ever is anterior to the discovery that all men are mortal and to the discovery that the thinker is himself a man. These discoveries flatly contradict that confidence, in the form in which it originally presents itself, and all doctrines of immortality which adult philosophy can entertain are more or less subterfuges and after-thoughts by which the observed fact of mortality and the native inconceivability of death are more or less clumsily reconciled.

The most lordly and genuine fashion of asserting immortality would be to proclaim one's self an exception to the animal race and to point out that the analogy between one's singular self and others is altogether lame and purely conventional. A solipsistic argument. Any proud barbarian, with a tincture of transcendental philosophy, might adopt this tone. "Creatures that perish," he might say, "are and can be nothing but puppets and painted shadows in my mind. My conscious will forbids its own extinction; it scorns to level itself with its own objects and instruments. The world, which I have never known to exist without me, exists by my co-operation and consent; it can never extinguish what lends it being. The death prophetically accepted by weaklings, with such small insight and courage, I mock and altogether defy: it can never touch me."

Such solipsistic boasts may not have been heard in historic times from the lips of men speaking in their own persons. Language has an irresistible tendency to make thought communistic and ideally transferable to others. It forbids a man to say of himself what it would be ridiculous to hear from another. Now solipsism in another man is a comic thing: and a mind, prompted perhaps by hell and heaven to speak solipsistically, is stopped by the laughable echo of its own words, when it remembers its bold sayings. Language, being social, resists a virgin egotism and forbids it to express itself publicly, no matter how well grounded it may be in transcendental logic and in animal instinct. Social convention is necessarily materialistic, since the beginning of all moral reasonableness consists in taming the transcendental conceit native to a living mind, in attaching it to its body, and bringing the will that thought itself absolute down to the rank of animals and men. Otherwise no man would acknowledge another's rights or even conceive his existence.

Primeval solipsism—the philosophy of untamed

animal will—has accordingly taken to the usual by-paths and expressed itself openly only in myth or by a speculative abstraction in which the transcendental spirit, for which all the solipsistic privileges were still claimed, was distinguished from the human individual.   The gods, it was said, were immortal; and although on earth spirit must submit to the yoke and service of matter, on whose occasions it must wait, yet there existed in the ether other creatures more normally and gloriously compounded, since their forms served and expressed their minds, which ruled also over the elements and feared no assault from time.   With the advent of this mythology experience and presumption divided their realms; experience was allowed to shape men's notions of vulgar reality, but presumption, which could not be silenced, was allowed to suggest a second sphere, thinly and momentarily veiled to mortal sense, in which the premonitions of will were abundantly realised.

Absoluteness and immortality transferred to the gods.

This expedient had the advantage of endowing the world with creatures that really satisfied human aspirations, such as at any moment they might be.   The gods possessed longevity, beauty, magic celerity of movement, leisure, splendour of life, indefinite strength, and practical omniscience.   When the gods were also expressions for natural forces, this function somewhat prejudiced their ideality, and they failed to correspond perfectly to what their worshippers would have most esteemed; but religious reformers tended to expunge naturalism from theology and to represent the gods as entirely admirable. The Greek gods, to be sure, always continued to have genealogies, and the fact of having been born is a bad augury for immortality; but other religions, and finally the Greek philosophers themselves, conceived unbegotten gods, in whom the human rebellion against mutability was expressed absolutely.

Thus a place was found in nature for the constant and perpetual element which crude experience seems to contain or at least to suggest. Unfortunately the immortal and the human were in this mythology wholly divorced, so that while immortality was vindicated for something in the universe it was emphatically denied to man and to his works. Contemplation, to be satisfied with this situation, had to be heroically unselfish and resigned; the gods' greatness and glory had to furnish sufficient solace for all mortal defeats. At the same time all criticism had to be deprecated, for reflection would at once have pointed out that the divine life in question was either a personification of natural processes and thus really in flux and full of oblivion and imperfection, or else a hypostasis of certain mental functions and ideals, which could not really be conceived apart from the natural human life which they informed and from which they had been violently abstracted.

Another expedient was accordingly found, especially by mystics and critical philosophers, for

Or to a divine principle in all beings.

uniting the mortal and immortal in existence while still distinguishing them in essence. *Cur Deus Homo* might be said to be the theme of all such speculations. Plato had already found the eternal in the form which the temporal puts on, or, if the phrase be preferred, had seen in the temporal and existential nothing but an individuated case of the ideal. The soul was immortal, unbegotten, impassible; the bodies it successively inhabited and the experience it gathered served merely to bring out its nature with greater or less completeness. To somewhat the same effect the German transcendentalists identified and distinguished the private and the universal spirit. What lived in each man and in each moment was the Absolute—for nothing else could really exist —and the expression which the Absolute there took on was but a transitional phase of its total self-expression, which, could it be grasped in its totality, would no longer seem subject to contradiction and flux. An immortal agent therefore went through an infinite series of acts, each transitory and relative to the others, but all possessed of inalienable reality and eternal significance. In such formulations the divorce was avoided between the intellectual and the sensuous factor in experience—a divorce which the myth about immortal gods and mortal men had introduced. On the other hand existential immortality was abandoned; only an ideal permanence, only significance, was allowed to any finite being, and the better or future world of which ancient poets had dreamt, Olympus, and every other heaven, was altogether abolished. There was an eternal universe where everything was transitory and a single immortal spirit at no two moments the same. The world of idealism realised no particular ideal, and least of all the ideal of a natural and personal immunity from death.

First, then, a man may refuse to admit that he must die at all; then, abashed at the arrogance of that assertion, he may consider the immortal life of other creatures, like the earth and stars, which seem subject to no extinction, and he may ascribe to these a perpetual consciousness and personality. Finally, confessing the fabulous character of those deities, he may distinguish an immortal agent or principle within himself, identify it with the inner principle of all other beings, and contrast it with its varying and conditioned expressions. But scarcely is this abstraction attained when he must perceive its worthlessness, since the natural life, the concrete aims, and the personal career which immortality was intended to save from dissolution are wholly alien to a nominal entity which endures through all change, however fundamental, and cohabits with every nature, however hostile and odious to humanity. If immor-

In neither case is the individual immortal.

tality is to be genuine, what is immortal must be something definite, and if this immortality is to concern life and not mere significance or ideal definition, that which endures must be an individual creature with a fixed nucleus of habits and demands, so that its persistence may contain progress and achievement.

Herewith we may dismiss the more direct attempts to conceive and assert a future life. Their failure drives us to a consideration of indirect attempts to establish an unobservable but real immortality through revelation and dogma. Such an immortality would follow on transmigration or resurrection, and would be assigned to a supernatural sphere, a second empirical world present to the soul after death, where her fortunes would not be really conceivable without a reconstituted body and a new material environment.

Many a man dies too soon and some are born in the wrong age or station. Could these persons drink at the fountain of youth at least once more they might do themselves fuller justice and cut a better figure at last in the universe. Most people think they have stuff in them for greater things than time suffers them to perform. To imagine a second career is a pleasing antidote for ill-fortune; the poor soul wants another chance. But how should a future life be constituted if it is to satisfy this demand, and how long need it last? It would evidently have to go on in an environment closely

Possible forms of survival.

analogous to earth; I could not, for instance, write
in another world the epics which the necessity of
earning my living may have stifled here, did that
other world contain no time, no heroic struggles,
or no metrical language. Nor is it clear that my
epics, to be perfect, would need to be quite endless. If what is foiled in me is really poetic
genius and not simply a tendency toward perpetual motion, it would not help me if in heaven,
in lieu of my dreamt-of epics, I were allowed to
beget several robust children. In a word, if here-
after I am to be the same man improved I must
find myself in the same world corrected. Were
I transformed into a cherub or transported into
a timeless ecstasy, it is hard to see in what sense
I should continue to exist. Those results might
be interesting in themselves and might enrich the
universe; they would not prolong my life nor re-
trieve my disasters.

For this reason a future life is after all best
represented by those frankly material ideals which
most Christians—being Platonists—are wont to
despise. It would be genuine happiness for a Jew
to rise again in the flesh and live for ever in
Ezekiel's New Jerusalem, with its ceremonial
glories and civic order. It would be truly agreeable for any man to sit in well-watered gardens
with Mohammed, clad in green silks, drinking delicious sherbets, and transfixed by the gazelle-like
glance of some young girl, all innocence and fire.
Amid such scenes a man might remain himself

and might fulfil hopes that he had actually cherished on earth. He might also find his friends again, which in somewhat generous minds is perhaps the thought that chiefly sustains interest in a posthumous existence. But to recognise his friends a man must find them in their bodies, with their familiar habits, voices, and interests; for it is surely an insult to affection to say that he could find them in an eternal formula expressing their idiosyncrasy. When, however, it is clearly seen that another life, to supplement this one, must closely resemble it, does not the magic of immortality altogether vanish? Is such a reduplication of earthly society at all credible? And the prospect of awakening again among houses and trees, among children and dotards, among wars and rumours of wars, still fettered to one personality and one accidental past, still uncertain of the future, is not this prospect wearisome and deeply repulsive? Having passed through these things once and bequeathed them to posterity, is it not time for each soul to rest? The universe doubtless contains all sorts of experiences, better and worse than the human; but it is idle to attribute to a particular man a life divorced from his circumstances and from his body.

Dogmas about such a posthumous experience **Arguments** find some shadowy support in various **from retribu-** **tion and need** illusions and superstitions that sur- **of opportunity.** round death, but they are developed into articulate prophecies chiefly by certain moral demands. One of these requires rewards and punishments more emphatic and sure than those which conduct meets with in this world. Another requires merely a more favourable and complete opportunity for the soul's development. Considerations like these are pertinent to moral philosophy. It touches the notion of duty whether an exact hedonistic retribution is to be demanded for what is termed merit and guilt: so that without such supernatural remuneration virtue, perhaps, would be discredited and deprived of a motive. It likewise touches the ideality and nobleness of life whether human aims can be realised satisfactorily only in the agent's singular person, so that the fruits of effort would be forthwith missed if the labourer himself should disappear.

To establish justice in the world and furnish an adequate incentive to virtue was once thought **Ignoble** the chief business of a future life. **temper of** The Hebraic religions somewhat over- **both.** reached themselves on these points: for the grotesque alternative between hell and heaven in the end only aggravated the injustice it.was meant to remedy. Life is unjust in that it subordinates individuals to a general mechanical law, and the deeper and longer hold fate has on the soul, the greater that injustice. A perpetual life would be a perpetual subjection to arbitrary power, while a last judgment would be but a last fatality. That hell may have fright-

ened a few villains into omitting a crime is perhaps credible; but the embarrassed silence which
the churches, in a more sensitive age, prefer to
maintain on that wholesome doctrine—once, as
they taught, the only rational basis for virtue—
shows how their teaching has to follow the independent progress of morals.   Nevertheless, persons are not wanting, apparently free from ecclesiastical constraint, who still maintain that the
value of life depends on its indefinite prolonga-
tion.   By an artifice of reflection they substitute
vanity for reason, and selfish for ingenuous instincts in man.   Being apparently interested in
nothing but their own careers, they forget that a
man may remember how little he counts in the
world and suffer that rational knowledge to inspire his purposes.   Intense morality has always
envisaged earthly goods and evils, and even when
a future life has been accepted vaguely, it has
never given direction to human will or aims,
which at best it could only proclaim more emphatically.   It may indeed be said that no man of
any depth of soul has made his prolonged existence the touchstone of his enthusiasms.   Such an
instinct is carnal, and if immortality is to add a
higher inspiration to life it must not be an immortality of selfishness.   What a despicable creature must a man be, and how sunk below the level
of the most barbaric virtue, if he cannot bear to
live for his children, for his art, or for country!
    To turn these moral questions, however, into

arguments for a physical speculation, like that
about human longevity, resurrection, or metempsy-
False opti- chosis, a hybrid principle is required:
mistic postu- thus, even if we have answered those
late involved. moral questions in the conventional
way and satisfied ourselves that personal immortality is a postulate of ethics, we cannot infer
that immortality therefore exists unless we import into the argument a tremendous optimistic
postulate, to the effect that what is requisite for
moral rationality must in every instance be realised in experience.

Such an optimistic postulate, however, as the
reader must have repeatedly observed, is made
not only despite all experience but in ignorance
of the conditions under which alone ideals are
framed and retain their significance. Every
ideal expresses individual and specific tendencies,
proper at some moment to some natural creature;
every ideal therefore has for its basis a part only
of the dynamic world, so that its fulfilment is
problematical and altogether adventitious to its
existence and authority. To decide whether an
ideal can be or will be fulfilled we must examine
the physical relation between such organic forces
as that ideal expresses and the environment in
which those forces operate; we may then perceive
how far a realisation of the given aims is possible, how far it must fail, and how far the aims
in question, by a shift in their natural basis, will
lapse and yield to others, possibly more capable

of execution and more stable in the world. The question of success is a question of physics. To say that an ideal will be inevitably fulfilled simply because it is an ideal is to say something gratuitous and foolish. Pretence cannot in the end avail against experience.

Nevertheless, it is important to define ideals even before their realisation is known to be possible, because they constitute one of the two factors whose interaction and adjustment is moral life, factors which are complementary and diverse in function and may be independently ascertained. The value of existences is wholly borrowed from their ideality, without direct consideration of their fate, while the existence of ideals is wholly determined by natural forces, without direct relation to their fulfilment. Existence and ideal value can therefore be initially felt and observed apart, although of course a complete description would lay bare physical necessity in the ideals entertained and inevitable ideal harmonies among the facts discovered. Human life, lying as it does in the midst of a larger process, will surely not be without some congruity with the universe. Every creature lends potential values to a world in which it can satisfy some at least of its demands and learn, perhaps, to modify the others. Happiness is always a natural and an essentially possible thing, and a total despair, since it ignores those goods which are attainable, can express only a partial experience.

Transition to ideality.

But before considering in what ways a disciplined soul might make its peace with reality, we may consider what an undisciplined soul in the first instance desires; and from this starting-point we may trace her chastening and education, observing the ideal compensations which may console her for lost illusions.

CHAPTER XIV

IDEAL IMMORTALITY

In order to give the will to live frank and direct satisfaction, it would have been necessary to solve *Olympian* the problem of perpetual motion in the *immortality* animal body, as nature has approxi*the first ideal.* mately solved it in the solar system. Nutrition should have continually repaired all waste, so that the cycle of youth and age might have repeated itself yearly in every individual, like summer and winter on the earth. Nor are some hints of such an equilibrium altogether wanting. Convalescence, sudden good fortune, a belated love, and even the April sunshine or morning air, bring about a certain rejuvenescence in man prophetic of what is not ideally impossible—perpetuity and constant reinforcement in his vital powers. Had nature furnished the elixir of life, or could art have discovered it, the whole face of human society would have been changed. The earth once full, no more children would have been begotten and parental instincts would have been atrophied for want of function. All men would have been contemporaries and, having all time before them for travel and experiment, would have allied themselves eventually with what was most congenial to

251

them and would have come to be bound only by free and friendly ties. They would all have been well known and would have acted perpetually in their ultimate and true character, like the immortal gods. One might have loved fixity, like Hestia, and another motion, like Hermes; a third might have been untiring in the plastic arts, like Hephæstus, or, like Apollo, in music; while the infinite realms of mathematics and philosophy would have lain open to spirits of a quality not represented in Homer's pantheon.

That man's primary and most satisfying ideal is something of this sort is clear in itself, and attested by mythology; for the great use of the gods is that they interpret the human heart to us, and help us, while we conceive them, to discover our inmost ambition and, while we emulate them, to pursue it. Christian fancy, because of its ascetic meagreness and fear of life, has not known how to fill out the picture of heaven and has left it mystical and vague; but whatever paradise it has ventured to imagine has been modelled on the same primary ideal. It has represented a society of eternal beings among which there was no marriage nor giving in marriage and where each found his congenial mansion and that perfected activity which brings inward peace.

After this easy fashion were death and birth conquered in the myths, which truly interpreted the will to live according to its primary intention, but in reality such direct satisfaction was impossi-

ble. A total defeat, on the other hand, would have
extinguished the will itself and obliterated every
human impulse seeking expression. Man's existence is proof enough that nature was not altogether
unpropitious, but offered, in an unlooked-for direction, some thoroughfare to the soul. Round-
about imperfect methods were discovered by which
something at least of what was craved might be
secured. The individual perished, yet not without
having segregated and detached a certain portion
of himself capable of developing a second body and
mind. The potentialities of this seminal portion,
having been liberated long after the parent body
had begun to feel the shock of the world, could
reach full expression after the parent body had
begun to decay; and the offspring needed not itself
to succumb before it had launched a third generation. A cyclical life or arrested death, a continual motion by little successive explosions, could
thus establish itself and could repeat from generation to generation a process not unlike nutrition; only that, while in nutrition the individual
form remains and the inner substance is renewed
insensibly, in reproduction the form is renewed
openly and the inner substance is insensibly continuous.

Reproduction seems, from the will's point of
Its indirect   view, a marvellous expedient involving
attainment   a curious mixture of failure and suc-
by reproduc-
tion.   cess. The individual, who alone is the
seat and principle of will, is thereby sacrificed,

so that reproduction is no response to his original
hopes and aspirations; yet in a double way he is
enticed and persuaded to be almost satisfied: first,
in that so like a counterfeit of himself actually
survives, a creature to which all his ideal interests
may be transmitted; and secondly, because a new
and as it were a rival aim is now insinuated into
his spirit. For the impulse toward reproduction
has now become no less powerful, even if less constant, than the impulse toward nutrition; in other
words, the will to live finds itself in the uncon-
genial yet inevitable company of the will to have
an heir. Reproduction thus partly entertains the
desire to be immortal by giving it a vicarious fulfilment, and partly cancels it by adding an impulse and joy which, when you think of it, accepts
mortality. For love, whether sexual, parental, or
fraternal, is essentially sacrificial, and prompts a
man to give his life for his friends. In thus
losing his life gladly he in a sense finds it anew,
since it has now become a part of his function and
ideal to yield his place to others and to live afterwards only in them. While the primitive and animal side of him may continue to cling to existence
at all hazards and to find the thought of extinction
intolerable, his reason and finer imagination will
build a new ideal on reality better understood, and
be content that the future he looks to should be
enjoyed by others. When we consider such a natural transformation and discipline of the will, when
we catch even a slight glimpse of nature's resources

and mysteries, how thin and verbal those belated hopes must seem which would elude death and abolish sacrifice! Such puerile dreams not only miss the whole pathos of human life, but ignore those specifically mortal virtues which might console us for not being so radiantly divine as we may at first have thought ourselves. Nature, in denying us perennial youth, has at least invited us to become unselfish and noble.

A first shift in aspiration, a capacity for radical altruism, thus supervenes upon the lust to live and accompanies parental and social interests. The new ideal, however, can never entirely obliterate the old and primary one, because the initial functions which the old Adam exclusively represented remain imbedded in the new life, and are its physical basis. If the nutritive soul ceased to operate, the reproductive soul could never arise; to be altruistic we must first be, and spiritual interests can never abolish or cancel the material existence on which they are grafted. The consequence is that death, even when circumvented by reproduction and relieved by surviving impersonal interests, remains an essential evil. It may be accepted as inevitable, and the goods its intrusion leaves standing may be heartily appreciated and pursued; but something pathetic and incomplete will always attach to a life that looks to its own termination.

The effort of physical existence is not to accomplish anything definite but merely to persist for ever. The will has its first law of motion, corre-

sponding to that of matter; its initial tendency is
to continue to operate in the given direction and
in the given manner. Inertia is, in this sense, the
essence of vitality. To be driven from that perpetual course is somehow to be checked, and an
external and hostile force is required to change
a habit or an instinct as much as to deflect a star.
Indeed, nutrition itself, hunting, feeding, and digestion, are forced activities, and the basis of passions not altogether congenial nor ideal. Hunger
is an incipient faintness and agony, and an animal
that needs to hunt, gnaw, and digest is no immortal, free, or essentially victorious creature. His
will is already driven into by-paths and expedients; his primitive beatific vision has to be interrupted by remedial action to restore it for a while,
since otherwise it would obviously degenerate rap-
idly through all stages of distress until its total
extinction.

The tasks thus imposed upon the protoplasmic
will raise it, we may say, to a higher level; to hunt
Moral is better sport, and more enlightening,
acceptance than to lie imbibing sunshine and air;
of this com-
promise. and to eat is, we may well think, a more
positive and specific pleasure than merely to be.
Such judgments, however, show a human bias.
They arise from incapacity to throw off acquired
organs. Those necessities which have led to the
forms of life which we happen to exemplify, and
in terms of which our virtues are necessarily expressed, seem to us, in retrospect, happy necessi-

ties, since without them our conventional goods would not have come to appeal to us. These conventional goods, however, are only compromises with evil, and the will would never have taken to pursuing them if it had not been dislodged and beaten back from its primary aims. Even food is, for this reason, no absolute blessing; it is only the first and most necessary of comforts, of restorations, of truces and reprieves in that battle with death in which an ultimate defeat is too plainly inevitable; for the pitcher that goes often to the well is at last broken, and a creature that is forced to resist his inward collapse by adventitious aids will some day find that these aids have failed him, and that inward dissolution has become, for some mechanical reason, quite irresistible. It is therefore not only the lazy or mystical will that chafes at the need of material supports and deprecates anxieties about the morrow; the most conventional and passionate mind, when it attains any refinement, confesses the essential servitude involved in such preoccupations by concealing or ignoring them as much as may be. We study to eat as if we were not ravenous, to win as if we were willing to lose, and to treat personal wants in general as merely compulsory and uninteresting matters. Why dwell, we say to ourselves, on our stammerings and failures? The intent is all, and the bungling circumlocutions we may be driven to should be courteously ignored, like a stammerer's troubles, when once our meaning has been conveyed.

Even animal passions are, in this way, after-
thoughts and expedients, and although in a brutal
age they seem to make up the whole of life, later
it appears that they would be gladly enough outgrown, did the material situation permit it. Intellectual life returns, in its freedom, to the attitude proper to primitive will, except that through
the new machinery underlying reason a more
stable equilibrium has been established with external forces, and the freedom originally absolute
has become relative to certain underlying adjustments, adjustments which may be ignored
but cannot be abandoned with impunity. Original action, as seen in the vegetable, is purely
spontaneous. On the animal level instrumental action is added and chiefly attended to, so
that the creature, without knowing what it lives
for, finds attractive tasks and a sort of glory in
the chase, in love, and in labour. In the Life of
Reason this instrumental activity is retained, for
it is a necessary basis for human prosperity and
power, but the value of life is again sought in the
supervening free activity which that adjustment
to physical forces, or dominion over them, has
made possible on a larger scale. Every free activity would gladly persist for ever; and if any be
found that involves and aims at its own arrest or
transformation, that activity is thereby proved to
be instrumental and servile, imposed from without
and not ideal.

Not only is man's original effort aimed at living

for ever in his own person, but, even if he could
renounce that desire, the dream of being repre-
Even   sented perpetually by posterity is no
vicarious   less doomed. Reproduction, like nu-
immortality
intrinsically   trition, is a device not ultimately suc-
impossible.   cessful. If extinction does not defeat
it, evolution will. Doubtless the fertility of whatever substance may have produced us will not be
exhausted in this single effort; a potentiality that
has once proved efficacious and been actualised in
life, though it should sleep, will in time revive
again. In some form and after no matter what
intervals, nature may be expected always to possess consciousness. But beyond this planet and
apart from the human race, experience is too little
imaginable to be interesting. No definite plan or
ideal of ours can find its realisation except in ourselves. Accordingly, a vicarious physical immortality always remains an unsatisfactory issue; what
is thus to be preserved is but a counterfeit of our
being, and even that counterfeit is confronted by
omens of a total extinction more or less remote.
A note of failure and melancholy must always
dominate in the struggle against natural death.

This defeat is not really problematical, or to be
eluded by reviving ill-digested hopes resting entirely on ignorance, an ignorance which these hopes
will wish to make eternal. We need not wait for
our total death to experience dying; we need not
borrow from observation of others' demise a prophecy of our own extinction. Every moment cele-

brates obsequies over the virtues of its predeces-
sor; and the possession of memory, by which we
somehow survive in representation, is the most unmistakable proof that we are perishing in reality.
In endowing us with memory, nature has revealed
to us a truth utterly unimaginable to the unflective
creation, the truth of mortality. Everything moves
in the midst of death, because it indeed *moves;*
but it falls into the pit unawares and by its
own action unmakes and disestablishes itself,
until a wonderful visionary faculty is added,
so that a ghost remains of what has perished to
reveal that lapse and at the same time in a certain
sense to neutralise it. The more we reflect, the
more we live in memory and idea, the more convinced and penetrated we shall be by the experience of death; yet, without our knowing it,
Intellectual perhaps, this very conviction and ex-
victory over perience will have raised us, in a way,
change. above mortality. That was a heroic and
divine oracle which, in informing us of our decay,
made us partners of the gods' eternity, and by
giving us knowledge poured into us, to that extent, the serenity and balm of truth. As it is
memory that enables us to feel that we are dying
and to know that everything actual is in flux, so it
is memory that opens to us an ideal immortality,
unacceptable and meaningless to the old Adam,
but genuine in its own way and undeniably true.
It is an immortality in representation—a representation which envisages things in their truth as

they have in their own day possessed themselves
in reality. It is no subterfuge or superstitious
effrontery, called to disguise or throw off the lessons of experience; on the contrary, it is experience
itself, reflection itself, and knowledge of mortality.
Memory does not reprieve or postpone the changes
which it registers, nor does it itself possess a permanent duration; it is, if possible, less stable and
more mobile than primary sensation. It is, in point
of existence, only an internal and complex kind of
sensibility. But in intent and by its significance
it plunges to the depths of time; it looks still on
the departed and bears witness to the truth that,
though absent from this part of experience, and
incapable of returning to life, they nevertheless
existed once in their own right, were as living and
actual as experience is to-day, and still help to
make up, in company with all past, present, and
future mortals, the filling and value of the world.

As the pathos and heroism of life consists in accepting as an opportunity the fate that makes our
own death, partial or total, serviceable to others,
so the glory of life consists in accepting the knowledge of natural death as an opportunity to live
in the spirit. The sacrifice, the self-surrender,
remains real; for, though the compensation is real,
too, and at moments, perhaps, apparently over-
whelming, it is always incomplete and leaves beneath an incurable sorrow. Yet life can never contradict its basis or reach satisfactions essentially
excluded by its own conditions. Progress lies in

moving forward from the given situation, and satisfying as well as may be the interests that exist.
And if some initial demand has proved hopeless,
there is the greater reason for cultivating other
sources of satisfaction, possibly more abundant and
lasting. Now, reflection is a vital function; memory and imagination have to the full the rhythm
and force of life. But these faculties, in envisaging
The glory the past or the ideal, envisage the eter-
of it. nal, and the man in whose mind they
predominate is to that extent detached in his affections from the world of flux, from himself, and
from his personal destiny. This detachment will
not make him infinitely long-lived, nor absolutely
happy, but it may render him intelligent and just,
and may open to him all intellectual pleasures and
all human sympathies.

There is accordingly an escape from death open
to man; one not found by circumventing nature,
but by making use of her own expedients in circumventing her imperfections. Memory, nay, perception itself, is a first stage in this escape, which
coincides with the acquisition and possession of
reason. When the meaning of successive perceptions is recovered with the last of them, when a
survey is made of objects whose constitutive sensations first arose independently, this synthetic moment contains an object raised above time on a
pedestal of reflection, a thought indefeasibly true
in its ideal deliverance, though of course fleeting
in its psychic existence. Existence is essentially

temporal and life foredoomed to be mortal, since
its basis is a process and an opposition; it floats in
the stream of time, never to return, never to be
recovered or repossessed. But ever since substance
became at some sensitive point intelligent and re-
flective, ever since time made room and pause for
memory, for history, for the consciousness of time,
a god, as it were, became incarnate in mortality
and some vision of truth, some self-forgetful satisfaction, became a heritage that moment could trans-
mit to moment and man to man. This heritage
is humanity itself, the presence of immortal reason
in creatures that perish. Apprehension, which
makes man so like a god, makes him in one respect
immortal; it quickens his numbered moments with
a vision of what never dies, the truth of those moments and their inalienable values.

To participate in this vision is to participate at
once in humanity and in divinity, since all other
Reason makes bonds are material and perishable, but
man's the bond between two thoughts that
divinity, have grasped the same truth, of two
instants that have caught the same beauty, is a
spiritual and imperishable bond. It is imperishable simply because it is ideal and resident merely
in import and intent. The two thoughts, the two
instants, remain existentially different; were they
not two they could not come from different quarters to unite in one meaning and to behold one
object in distinct and conspiring acts of apprehension. Being independent in existence, they can

be united by the identity of their burden, by the common worship, so to speak, of the same god. Were this ideal goal itself an existence, it would be incapable of uniting anything; for the same gulf which separated the two original minds would open between them and their common object. But being, as it is, purely ideal, it can become the meeting-ground of intelligences and render their union ideally eternal. Among the physical instruments of thought there may be rivalry and impact—the two thinkers may compete and clash—but this is because each seeks his own physical survival and does not love the truth stripped of its accidental associations and provincial accent. Doctors disagree in so far as they are not truly doctors, but, as Plato would say, seek, like sophists and wage-earners, to circumvent and defeat one another. The conflict is physical and can extend to the subject-matter only in so far as this is tainted by individual prejudice and not wholly lifted from the sensuous to the intellectual plane. In the ether there are no winds of doctrine. The intellect, being the organ and source of the divine, is divine and single; if there were many sorts of intellect, many principles of perspective, they would fix and create incomparable and irrelevant worlds. Reason is one in that it gravitates toward an object, called truth, which could not have the function it has, of being a focus for mental activities, if it were not one in reference to the operations which converge upon it.

This unity in truth, as in reason, is of course functional only, not physical or existential. The beats of thought and the thinkers are innumerable; indefinite, too, the variations to which their endowment and habits may be subjected. But the condition of spiritual communion or ideal relevance in these intelligences is their possession of a method and grammar essentially identical. Language, for example, is significant in proportion to the constancy in meaning which words and locutions preserve in a speaker's mind at various times, or in the minds of various persons. This constancy is never absolute. Therefore language is never wholly significant, never exhaustively intelligible. There is always mud in the well, if we have drawn up enough water. Yet in peaceful rivers, though they flow, there is an appreciable degree of translucency. So, from moment to moment, and from man to man, there is an appreciable element of unanimity, of constancy and congruity of intent. On this abstract and perfectly identical function science rests together with every rational formation.

The same function is the seat of human immortality. Reason lifts a larger or smaller element in **and his** each man to the plane of ideality ac- **immortality.** cording as reason more or less thoroughly leavens and permeates the lump. No man is wholly immortal, as no philosophy is wholly true and no language wholly intelligible; but only in so far as intelligible is a language a language rather than a noise, only in so far as true is a philosophy more than a vent for cerebral humours, and only in so far as a man is rational and immortal is he a man and not a sensorium.

It is hard to convince people that they have such a gift as intelligence. If they perceive its animal basis they cannot conceive its ideal affinities or understand what is meant by calling it divine; if they perceive its ideality and see the immortal essences that swim into its ken, they hotly deny that it is an animal faculty, and invent ultramundane places and bodiless persons in which it is to reside; as if those celestial substances could be, in respect to thought, any less material than matter or, in respect to vision and life, any less instrumental than bodily organs. It never occurs to them that if nature has added intelligence to animal life it is because they belong together. Intelligence is a natural emanation of vitality. If eternity could exist otherwise than as a vision in time, eternity would have no meaning for men in the world, while the world, men, and time would have no vocation or status in eternity. The travail of existence would be without excuse, without issue or consummation, while the conceptions of truth and of perfection would be without application to experience, pure dreams about things preternatural and unreal, vacantly conceived, and illogically supposed to have something to do with living issues. But truth and perfection, for the very reason that they are not problematic existences but inherent ideals, cannot be banished from discourse. Experience may lose any of its data; it cannot lose, while it endures, the terms with which it operates in becoming experience. Now, truth is relevant to every opinion which looks to truth for its standard, and perfection is envisaged in every cry for relief, in every effort at betterment. Opinions, volitions, and passionate refusals fill human life. So that when the existence of truth is denied, truth is given the only status which it ever required—it is conceived.

Nor can any better defense be found for the denial that nature and her life have a status in

It is the locus of all truths.

eternity. This statement may not be understood, but if grasped at all it will not be questioned. By having a status in eternity is not meant being parts of an eternal existence, petrified or congealed into something real but motionless. What is meant is only that whatever exists in time, when bathed in the light of reflection, acquires an indelible character and discloses irreversible relations; every fact, in being recognised, takes its place in the universe of discourse, in that ideal sphere of truth which is the common and unchanging standard for all assertions. Language, science, art, religion, and all ambitious dreams are compacted of ideas. Life is as much a mosaic of notions as the firmament is of stars; and these ideal and transpersonal objects, bridging time, fixing standards, establishing values, constituting the natural rewards of all liv-

ing, are the very furniture of eternity, the goals
and playthings of that reason which is an instinct
in the heart as vital and spontaneous as any other.
Or rather, perhaps, reason is a supervening instinct
by which all other instincts are interpreted, just
as the *sensus communis* or transcendental unity of
psychology is a faculty by which all perceptions
are brought face to face and compared. So that
immortality is not a privilege reserved for a part
only of experience, but rather a relation pervading
every part in varying measure. We may, in leav-
ing the subject, mark the degrees and phases of
this idealisation.

Animal sensation is related to eternity only by
the truth that it has taken place. The fact, fleeting as it is, is registered in ideal history, and no inventory of the world's
riches, no true confession of its crimes,
would ever be complete that ignored
that incident. This indefeasible character in experience makes a first sort of ideal immortality,
one on which those rational philosophers like to
dwell who have not speculation enough to feel
quite certain of any other. It was a consolation
to the Epicurean to remember that, however brief
and uncertain might be his tenure of delight, the
past was safe and the present sure. " He lives
happy," says Horace, " and master over himself,
who can say daily, I have lived. To-morrow let
Jove cover the sky with black clouds or flood
it with sunshine; he shall not thereby render

*Epicurean
immortality,
through the
truth
of existence.*

vain what lies behind, he shall not delete and make never to have existed what once the hour has brought in its flight." Such self-concentration and hugging of the facts has no power to improve them; it gives to pleasure and pain an impartial eternity, and rather tends to intrench in sensuous and selfish satisfactions a mind that has lost faith in reason and that deliberately ignores the difference in scope and dignity which exists among various pursuits. Yet the reflection is staunch and in its way heroic; it meets a vague and feeble aspiration, that looks to the infinite, with a just rebuke; it points to real satisfactions, experienced successes, and asks us to be content with the fulfilment of our own wills. If you have seen the world, if you have played your game and won it, what more would you ask for? If you have tasted the sweets of existence, you should be satisfied; if the experience has been bitter, you should be glad that it comes to an end.

Of course, as we have seen, there is a primary demand in man which death and mutation contradict flatly, so that no summons to cease can ever be obeyed with complete willingness. Even the suicide trembles and the ascetic feels the stings of the flesh. It is the part of philosophy, however, to pass over those natural repugnances and overlay them with as much countervailing rationality as can find lodgment in a particular mind. The Epicurean, having abandoned politics and religion and being afraid of any far-reaching ambition, applied philosophy honestly enough to what remained. Simple and healthy pleasures are the reward of simple and healthy pursuits; to chafe against them because they are limited is to import a foreign and disruptive element into the case; a healthy hunger has its limit, and its satisfaction reaches a natural term. Philosophy, far from alienating us from those values, should teach us to see their perfection and to maintain them in our ideal. In other words, the happy filling of a single hour is so much gained for the universe at large, and to find joy and sufficiency in the flying moment is perhaps the only means open to us for increasing the glory of eternity.

Moving events, while remaining enshrined in this fashion in their permanent setting, may con-

Logical immortality, through objects of thought. tain other and less external relations to the immutable. They may represent it. If the pleasures of sense are not cancelled when they cease, but continue to satisfy reason in that they once satisfied natural desires, much more will the pleasures of reflection retain their worth, when we consider that what they aspired to and reached was no momentary physical equilibrium but a permanent truth. As Archimedes, measuring the hypothenuse, was lost to events, being engaged in an event of much greater transcendence, so art and science interrupt the sense for change by engrossing attention in its issues and its laws. Old age often turns pious to look away from ruins to some world where youth

endures and where what ought to have been is not
overtaken by decay before it has quite come to
maturity. Lost in such abstract contemplations,
the mind is weaned from mortal concerns. It forgets for a few moments a world in which it has
so little more to do and so much, perhaps, still
to suffer. As a sensation of pure light would not
be distinguishable from light itself, so a contemplation of things not implicating time in their
structure becomes, so far as its own deliverance
goes, a timeless existence. Unconsciousness of
temporal conditions and of the very flight of time
makes the thinker sink for a moment into identity
with timeless objects. And so immortality, in a
second ideal sense, touches the mind.

The transitive phases of consciousness, however,
have themselves a reference to eternal things.
Ethical They yield a generous enthusiasm and
immortality, love of good which is richer in conso-
through lation than either Epicurean self-con-
types of centration or mathematical ecstasy.
excellence.
Events are more interesting than the terms we
abstract from them, and the forward movement
of the will is something more intimately real than
is the catalogue of our past experiences. Now the
forward movement of the will is an avenue to the
eternal. What would you have? What is the goal
of your endeavour? It must be some success, the
establishment of some order, the expression of
some experience. These points once reached, we
are not left merely with the satisfaction of ab-

stract success or the consciousness of ideal immortality. Being natural goals, these ideals are related to natural functions. Their attainment does not exhaust but merely liberates, in this instance, the function concerned, and so marks the perpetual point of reference common to that function in all its fluctuations. Every attainment of perfection in an art—as for instance in government—makes a return to perfection easier for posterity, since there remains an enlightening example, together with faculties predisposed by discipline to recover their ancient virtue. The better a man evokes and realises the ideal the more he leads the life that all others, in proportion to their worth, will seek to live after him, and the more he helps them to live in that nobler fashion. His presence in the society of immortals thus becomes, so to speak, more pervasive. He not only vanquishes time by his own rationality, living now in the eternal, but he continually lives again in all rational beings.

Since the ideal has this perpetual pertinence to mortal struggles, he who lives in the ideal and leaves it expressed in society or in art enjoys a double immortality. The eternal has absorbed him while he lived, and when he is dead his influence brings others to the same absorption, making them, through that ideal identity with the best in him, reincarnations and perennial seats of all in him which he could rationally hope to rescue from destruction. He can say, without any subterfuge or desire to delude himself, that he shall not wholly die; for he will have a better notion than the vulgar of what constitutes his being. By becoming the spectator and confessor of his own death and of universal mutation, he will have identified himself with what is spiritual in all spirits and masterful in all apprehension; and so conceiving himself, he may truly feel and know that he is eternal.

CHAPTER XV

CONCLUSION

The preceding analysis of religion, although it
is illustrated mainly by Christianity, may enable
us in a general way to distinguish the rational
goal of all religious life. In no sphere is the contrast clearer between wisdom and folly; in none,
perhaps, has there been so much of both. It was
The failure a prodigious delusion to imagine that
of magic, work could be done by magic; and
the desperate appeal which human weakness has
made to prayer, to castigations, to miscellaneous
fantastic acts, in the hope of thereby bending
nature to greater sympathy with human necessities, is a pathetic spectacle; all the more pathetic
in that here the very importunity of evil, which
distracted the mind and allowed it no choice or
deliberation, prevented very often those practical
measures which, if lighted upon, would have instantly relieved the situation. Religion when it
has tried to do man's work for him has not only
cheated hope, but consumed energy and drawn
away attention from the true means of success.

No less useless and retarding has been the

effort to give religion the function of science.
Mythology, in excogitating hidden dramatic causes
and of   for natural phenomena, or in attrib-
mythology.   uting events to the human values
which they might prevent or secure, has profoundly perverted and confused the intellect; it
has delayed and embarrassed the discovery of
natural forces, at the same time fostering pre-
sumptions which, on being exploded, tended to
plunge men, by revulsion, into an artificial despair. At the same time this experiment in
Their   mythology involved wonderful crea-
imaginative   tions which have a poetic value of
value.   their own, to offset their uselessness in
some measure and the obstruction they have occasioned. In imagining human agents behind
every appearance fancy has given appearances
some kinship to human life; it has made nature
a mass of hieroglyphics and enlarged to that extent the means of human expression. While objects and events were capriciously moralised, the
mind's own plasticity has been developed by its
great exercise in self-projection. To imagine
himself a thunder-cloud or a river, the dispenser
of silent benefits and the contriver of deep-
seated universal harmonies, has actually stimulated man's moral nature: he has grown larger by
thinking himself so large.

Through the dense cloud of false thought and
bad habit in which religion thus wrapped the
world, some rays broke through from the begin-

ning; for mythology and magic expressed life
and sought to express its conditions. Human
needs and human ideals went forth in these forms
to solicit and to conquer the world; and since
these imaginative methods, for their very ineptitude, rode somewhat lightly over particular issues
and envisaged rather distant goods, it was possible through them to give aspiration and reflection
greater scope than the meaner exigencies of life
would have permitted. Where custom ruled morals and a narrow empiricism bounded the field of
knowledge, it was partly a blessing that imagination should be given an illegitimate sway. Without misunderstanding, there might have been no
understanding at all; without confidence in supernatural support, the heart might never have
uttered its own oracles. So that in close associa-
tion with superstition and fable we find piety and
spirituality entering the world.

Rational religion has these two phases: piety,
or loyalty to necessary conditions, and spirituality, or devotion to ideal ends. These
Piety and simple sanctities make the core of all
spirituality the others. Piety drinks at the deep,
justified. elemental sources of power and order: it studies
nature, honours the past, appropriates and continues its mission. Spirituality uses the strength
thus acquired, remodelling all it receives, and
looking to the future and the ideal. True religion
is entirely human and political, as was that of the
ancient Hebrews, Romans, and Greeks. Super-

natural machinery is either symbolic of natural conditions and moral aims or else is worthless.

There is one other phase or possible overtone of religion about which a word might be added in Mysticism a conclusion. What is called mysticism primordial is a certain genial loosening of con-state of feeling. vention, whether rational or mythical; the mystic smiles at science and plays with theology, undermining both by force of his insight and inward assurance. He is all faith, all love, all vision, but he is each of these things *in vacuo,* and in the absence of any object.

Mysticism can exist, in varied degrees, at any stage of rational development. Its presence is therefore no indication of the worth or worthlessness of its possessor. This circumstance tends to obscure its nature, which would otherwise be obvious enough. Seeing the greatest saints and philosophers grow mystical in their highest flights, an innocent observer might imagine that mysticism was an ultimate attitude, which only his own incapacity kept him from understanding. But exactly the opposite is the case. Mysticism is the most primitive of feelings and only visits formed minds in moments of intellectual arrest and dissolution. It can exist in a child, very likely in an animal; indeed, to parody a phrase of Hegel's, the only pure mystics are the brutes. When articulation fails in the face of experience; when instinct guides without kindling any prophetic idea to which action may be inwardly re-

ferred; when life and hope and joy flow through
the soul from an unknown region to an unknown
end, then consciousness is mystical. Such an experience may suffuse the best equipped mind, if
its primordial energies, its will and emotions,
much outrun its intelligence. Just as at the beginning pure inexperience may flounder intellec-
tually and yet may have a sense of not going
astray, a sense of being carried by earth and sky,
by contagion and pleasure, into its animal paradise; so at the end, if the vegetative forces still
predominate, all articulate experience may be
lifted up and carried down-stream bodily by the
elementary flood rising from beneath.

Every religion, all science, all art, is accordingly subject to incidental mysticism; but in no
It may recur   case can mysticism stand alone and be
at any stage   the body or basis of anything. In the
of culture.   Life of Reason it is, if I may say so, a
normal disease, a recurrent manifestation of lost
equilibrium and interrupted growth; but in
these pauses, when the depths rise to the surface
and obliterate what scratches culture may have
made there, the rhythm of life may be more powerfully felt, and the very disappearance of intellect may be taken for a revelation. Both in a social and a psychological sense revelations come
from beneath, like earthquakes and volcanic erup-
tions; and while they fill the spirit with contempt for those fragile structures which they so
easily overwhelm, they are utterly incapable of

raising anything on the ruins. If they leave something standing it is only by involuntary accident, and if they prepare the soil for anything, it is commonly only for wild-flowers and weeds. Revelations are seldom beneficent, therefore, unless there is more evil in the world to destroy than good to preserve; and mysticism, under the same circumstances, may also liberate and relieve the spirit.

The feelings which in mysticism rise to the surface and speak in their own name are simply the ancient, overgrown feelings of vitality, dependence, inclusion; they are the background of consciousness coming forward and blotting out the scene. What mysticism destroys is, in a sense, its only legitimate expression. The Life of Reason, in so far as it is life, contains the mystic's primordial assurances, and his rudimentary joys; **Form gives substance its life and value.** but in so far as it is rational it has discovered what those assurances rest on, in what direction they may be trusted to support action and thought; and it has given those joys distinction and connexion, turning a dumb momentary ecstasy into a many-coloured and natural happiness.

A CATALOGUE OF
SELECTED DOVER BOOKS
IN ALL FIELDS OF INTEREST

A CATALOGUE OF SELECTED DOVER
BOOKS IN ALL FIELDS OF INTEREST

RACKHAM'S COLOR ILLUSTRATIONS FOR WAGNER'S RING. Rackham's finest mature work—all 64 full-color watercolors in a faithful and lush interpretation of the *Ring*. Full-sized plates on coated stock of the paintings used by opera companies for authentic staging of Wagner. Captions aid in following complete Ring cycle. Introduction. 64 illustrations plus vignettes. 72pp. 8⅝ x 11¼.   23779-6 Pa. $6.00

CONTEMPORARY POLISH POSTERS IN FULL COLOR, edited by Joseph Czestochowski. 46 full-color examples of brilliant school of Polish graphic design, selected from world's first museum (near Warsaw) dedicated to poster art. Posters on circuses, films, plays, concerts all show cosmopolitan influences, free imagination. Introduction. 48pp. 9⅜ x 12¼.
                                                        23780-X Pa. $6.00

GRAPHIC WORKS OF EDVARD MUNCH, Edvard Munch. 90 haunting, evocative prints by first major Expressionist artist and one of the greatest graphic artists of his time: *The Scream, Anxiety, Death Chamber, The Kiss, Madonna,* etc. Introduction by Alfred Werner. 90pp. 9 x 12.
                                                        23765-6 Pa. $5.00

THE GOLDEN AGE OF THE POSTER, Hayward and Blanche Cirker. 70 extraordinary posters in full colors, from Maitres de l'Affiche, Mucha, Lautrec, Bradley, Cheret, Beardsley, many others. Total of 78pp. 9⅜ x 12¼.   22753-7 Pa. $5.95

THE NOTEBOOKS OF LEONARDO DA VINCI, edited by J. P. Richter. Extracts from manuscripts reveal great genius; on painting, sculpture, anatomy, sciences, geography, etc. Both Italian and English. 186 ms. pages reproduced, plus 500 additional drawings, including studies for *Last Supper,* Sforza monument, etc. 860pp. 7⅞ x 10¾. (Available in U.S. only)
                               22572-0, 22573-9 Pa., Two-vol. set $15.90

THE CODEX NUTTALL, as first edited by Zelia Nuttall. Only inexpensive edition, in full color, of a pre-Columbian Mexican (Mixtec) book. 88 color plates show kings, gods, heroes, temples, sacrifices. New explanatory, historical introduction by Arthur G. Miller. 96pp. 11⅜ x 8½. (Available in U.S. only)   23168-2 Pa. $7.95

UNE SEMAINE DE BONTÉ, A SURREALISTIC NOVEL IN COLLAGE, Max Ernst. Masterpiece created out of 19th-century periodical illustrations, explores worlds of terror and surprise. Some consider this Ernst's greatest work. 208pp. 8⅛ x 11.   23252-2 Pa. $6.00

DRAWINGS OF WILLIAM BLAKE, William Blake. 92 plates from Book of Job, *Divine Comedy, Paradise Lost*, visionary heads, mythological figures, Laocoon, etc. Selection, introduction, commentary by Sir Geoffrey Keynes. 178pp. 8⅛ x 11. 22303-5 Pa. $4.00

ENGRAVINGS OF HOGARTH, William Hogarth. 101 of Hogarth's greatest works: *Rake's Progress, Harlot's Progress, Illustrations for Hudibras, Before and After, Beer Street and Gin Lane*, many more. Full commentary. 256pp. 11 x 13¾. 22479-1 Pa. $12.95

DAUMIER: 120 GREAT LITHOGRAPHS, Honore Daumier. Wide-ranging collection of lithographs by the greatest caricaturist of the 19th century. Concentrates on eternally popular series on lawyers, on married life, on liberated women, etc. Selection, introduction, and notes on plates by Charles F. Ramus. Total of 158pp. 9⅜ x 12¼. 23512-2 Pa. $6.00

DRAWINGS OF MUCHA, Alphonse Maria Mucha. Work reveals draftsman of highest caliber: studies for famous posters and paintings, renderings for book illustrations and ads, etc. 70 works, 9 in color; including 6 items not drawings. Introduction. List of illustrations. 72pp. 9⅜ x 12¼. (Available in U.S. only) 23672-2 Pa. $4.00

GIOVANNI BATTISTA PIRANESI: DRAWINGS IN THE PIERPONT MORGAN LIBRARY, Giovanni Battista Piranesi. For first time ever all of Morgan Library's collection, world's largest. 167 illustrations of rare Piranesi drawings—archeological, architectural, decorative and visionary. Essay, detailed list of drawings, chronology, captions. Edited by Felice Stampfle. 144pp. 9⅜ x 12¼. 23714-1 Pa. $7.50

NEW YORK ETCHINGS (1905-1949), John Sloan. All of important American artist's N.Y. life etchings. 67 works include some of his best art; also lively historical record—Greenwich Village, tenement scenes. Edited by Sloan's widow. Introduction and captions. 79pp. 8⅜ x 11¼. 23651-X Pa. $4.00

CHINESE PAINTING AND CALLIGRAPHY: A PICTORIAL SURVEY, Wan-go Weng. 69 fine examples from John M. Crawford's matchless private collection: landscapes, birds, flowers, human figures, etc., plus calligraphy. Every basic form included: hanging scrolls, handscrolls, album leaves, fans, etc. 109 illustrations. Introduction. Captions. 192pp. 8⅞ x 11¾. 23707-9 Pa. $7.95

DRAWINGS OF REMBRANDT, edited by Seymour Slive. Updated Lippmann, Hofstede de Groot edition, with definitive scholarly apparatus. All portraits, biblical sketches, landscapes, nudes, Oriental figures, classical studies, together with selection of work by followers. 550 illustrations. Total of 630pp. 9⅛ x 12¼. 21485-0, 21486-9 Pa., Two-vol. set $15.00

THE DISASTERS OF WAR, Francisco Goya. 83 etchings record horrors of Napoleonic wars in Spain and war in general. Reprint of 1st edition, plus 3 additional plates. Introduction by Philip Hofer. 97pp. 9⅜ x 8¼. 21872-4 Pa. $4.00

THE EARLY WORK OF AUBREY BEARDSLEY, Aubrey Beardsley. 157 plates, 2 in color: *Manon Lescaut, Madame Bovary, Morte Darthur, Salome,* other. Introduction by H. Marillier. 182pp. 8⅛ x 11. 21816-3 Pa. $4.50

THE LATER WORK OF AUBREY BEARDSLEY, Aubrey Beardsley. Exotic masterpieces of full maturity: *Venus and Tannhauser, Lysistrata, Rape of the Lock, Volpone,* Savoy material, etc. 174 plates, 2 in color. 186pp. 8⅛ x 11. 21817-1 Pa. $5.95

THOMAS NAST'S CHRISTMAS DRAWINGS, Thomas Nast. Almost all Christmas drawings by creator of image of Santa Claus as we know it, and one of America's foremost illustrators and political cartoonists. 66 illustrations. 3 illustrations in color on covers. 96pp. 8⅜ x 11¼.
23660-9 Pa. $3.50

THE DORÉ ILLUSTRATIONS FOR DANTE'S DIVINE COMEDY, Gustave Doré. All 135 plates from Inferno, Purgatory, Paradise; fantastic tortures, infernal landscapes, celestial wonders. Each plate with appropriate (translated) verses. 141pp. 9 x 12. 23231-X Pa. $4.50

DORÉ'S ILLUSTRATIONS FOR RABELAIS, Gustave Doré. 252 striking illustrations of *Gargantua and Pantagruel* books by foremost 19th-century illustrator. Including 60 plates, 192 delightful smaller illustrations. 153pp. 9 x 12. 23656-0 Pa. $5.00

LONDON: A PILGRIMAGE, Gustave Doré, Blanchard Jerrold. Squalor, riches, misery, beauty of mid-Victorian metropolis; 55 wonderful plates, 125 other illustrations, full social, cultural text by Jerrold. 191pp. of text. 9⅜ x 12¼. 22306-X Pa. $7.00

THE RIME OF THE ANCIENT MARINER, Gustave Doré, S. T. Coleridge. Dore's finest work, 34 plates capture moods, subtleties of poem. Full text. Introduction by Millicent Rose. 77pp. 9¼ x 12. 22305-1 Pa. $3.50

THE DORE BIBLE ILLUSTRATIONS, Gustave Doré. All wonderful, detailed plates: Adam and Eve, Flood, Babylon, Life of Jesus, etc. Brief King James text with each plate. Introduction by Millicent Rose. 241 plates. 241pp. 9 x 12. 23004-X Pa. $6.00

THE COMPLETE ENGRAVINGS, ETCHINGS AND DRYPOINTS OF ALBRECHT DURER. "Knight, Death and Devil"; "Melencolia," and more—all Dürer's known works in all three media, including 6 works formerly attributed to him. 120 plates. 235pp. 8⅜ x 11¼.
22851-7 Pa. $6.50

MECHANICK EXERCISES ON THE WHOLE ART OF PRINTING, Joseph Moxon. First complete book (1683-4) ever written about typography, a compendium of everything known about printing at the latter part of 17th century. Reprint of 2nd (1962) Oxford Univ. Press edition. 74 illustrations. Total of 550pp. 6⅛ x 9¼. 23617-X Pa. $7.95

CATALOGUE OF DOVER BOOKS

THE COMPLETE WOODCUTS OF ALBRECHT DURER, edited by Dr. W. Kurth. 346 in all: "Old Testament," "St. Jerome," "Passion," "Life of Virgin," Apocalypse," many others. Introduction by Campbell Dodgson. 285pp. 8½ x 12¼. 21097-9 Pa. $7.50

DRAWINGS OF ALBRECHT DURER, edited by Heinrich Wolfflin. 81 plates show development from youth to full style. Many favorites; many new. Introduction by Alfred Werner. 96pp. 8⅛ x 11. 22352-3 Pa. $5.00

THE HUMAN FIGURE, Albrecht Dürer. Experiments in various techniques—stereometric, progressive proportional, and others. Also life studies that rank among finest ever done. Complete reprinting of *Dresden Sketchbook*. 170 plates. 355pp. 8⅜ x 11¼. 21042-1 Pa. $7.95

OF THE JUST SHAPING OF LETTERS, Albrecht Dürer. Renaissance artist explains design of Roman majuscules by geometry, also Gothic lower and capitals. Grolier Club edition. 43pp. 7⅞ x 10¾ 21306-4 Pa. $3.00

TEN BOOKS ON ARCHITECTURE, Vitruvius. The most important book ever written on architecture. Early Roman aesthetics, technology, classical orders, site selection, all other aspects. Stands behind everything since. Morgan translation. 331pp. 5⅜ x 8½. 20645-9 Pa. $4.50

THE FOUR BOOKS OF ARCHITECTURE, Andrea Palladio. 16th-century classic responsible for Palladian movement and style. Covers classical architectural remains, Renaissance revivals, classical orders, etc. 1738 Ware English edition. Introduction by A. Placzek. 216 plates. 110pp. of text. 9½ x 12¾. 21308-0 Pa. $10.00

HORIZONS, Norman Bel Geddes. Great industrialist stage designer, "father of streamlining," on application of aesthetics to transportation, amusement, architecture, etc. 1932 prophetic account; function, theory, specific projects. 222 illustrations. 312pp. 7⅞ x 10¾. 23514-9 Pa. $6.95

FRANK LLOYD WRIGHT'S FALLINGWATER, Donald Hoffmann. Full, illustrated story of conception and building of Wright's masterwork at Bear Run, Pa. 100 photographs of site, construction, and details of completed structure. 112pp. 9¼ x 10. 23671-4 Pa. $5.50

THE ELEMENTS OF DRAWING, John Ruskin. Timeless classic by great Viltorian; starts with basic ideas, works through more difficult. Many practical exercises. 48 illustrations. Introduction by Lawrence Campbell. 228pp. 5⅜ x 8½. 22730-8 Pa. $3.75

GIST OF ART, John Sloan. Greatest modern American teacher, Art Students League, offers innumerable hints, instructions, guided comments to help you in painting. Not a formal course. 46 illustrations. Introduction by Helen Sloan. 200pp. 5⅜ x 8½. 23435-5 Pa. $4.00

CATALOGUE OF DOVER BOOKS

THE ANATOMY OF THE HORSE, George Stubbs. Often considered the great masterpiece of animal anatomy. Full reproduction of 1766 edition, plus prospectus; original text and modernized text. 36 plates. Introduction by Eleanor Garvey. 121pp. 11 x 14¾. 23402-9 Pa. $6.00

BRIDGMAN'S LIFE DRAWING, George B. Bridgman. More than 500 illustrative drawings and text teach you to abstract the body into its major masses, use light and shade, proportion; as well as specific areas of anatomy, of which Bridgman is master. 192pp. 6½ x 9¼. (Available in U.S. only) 22710-3 Pa. $3.50

ART NOUVEAU DESIGNS IN COLOR, Alphonse Mucha, Maurice Verneuil, Georges Auriol. Full-color reproduction of *Combinaisons ornementales* (c. 1900) by Art Nouveau masters. Floral, animal, geometric, interlacings, swashes—borders, frames, spots—all incredibly beautiful. 60 plates, hundreds of designs. 9⅜ x 8-1/16. 22885-1 Pa. $4.00

FULL-COLOR FLORAL DESIGNS IN THE ART NOUVEAU STYLE, E. A. Seguy. 166 motifs, on 40 plates, from *Les fleurs et leurs applications decoratives* (1902): borders, circular designs, repeats, allovers, "spots." All in authentic Art Nouveau colors. 48pp. 9⅜ x 12¼. 23439-8 Pa. $5.00

A DIDEROT PICTORIAL ENCYCLOPEDIA OF TRADES AND INDUSTRY, edited by Charles C. Gillispie. 485 most interesting plates from the great French Encyclopedia of the 18th century show hundreds of working figures, artifacts, process, land and cityscapes; glassmaking, papermaking, metal extraction, construction, weaving, making furniture, clothing, wigs, dozens of other activities. Plates fully explained. 920pp. 9 x 12. 22284-5, 22285-3 Clothbd., Two-vol. set $40.00

HANDBOOK OF EARLY ADVERTISING ART, Clarence P. Hornung. Largest collection of copyright-free early and antique advertising art ever compiled. Over 6,000 illustrations, from Franklin's time to the 1890's for special effects, novelty. Valuable source, almost inexhaustible.
Pictorial Volume. Agriculture, the zodiac, animals, autos, birds, Christmas, fire engines, flowers, trees, musical instruments, ships, games and sports, much more. Arranged by subject matter and use. 237 plates. 288pp. 9 x 12. 20122-8 Clothbd. $14.50

Typographical Volume. Roman and Gothic faces ranging from 10 point to 300 point, "Barnum," German and Old English faces, script, logotypes, scrolls and flourishes, 1115 ornamental initials, 67 complete alphabets, more. 310 plates. 320pp. 9 x 12. 20123-6 Clothbd. $15.00

CALLIGRAPHY (CALLIGRAPHIA LATINA), J. G. Schwandner. High point of 18th-century ornamental calligraphy. Very ornate initials, scrolls, borders, cherubs, birds, lettered examples. 172pp. 9 x 13. 20475-8 Pa. $7.00

CATALOGUE OF DOVER BOOKS

ART FORMS IN NATURE, Ernst Haeckel. Multitude of strangely beautiful natural forms: Radiolaria, Foraminifera, jellyfishes, fungi, turtles, bats, etc. All 100 plates of the 19th-century evolutionist's *Kunstformen der Natur* (1904). 100pp. 9⅜ x 12¼. 22987-4 Pa. $5.00

CHILDREN: A PICTORIAL ARCHIVE FROM NINETEENTH-CENTURY SOURCES, edited by Carol Belanger Grafton. 242 rare, copyright-free wood engravings for artists and designers. Widest such selection available. All illustrations in line. 119pp. 8⅜ x 11¼. 23694-3 Pa. $4.00

WOMEN: A PICTORIAL ARCHIVE FROM NINETEENTH-CENTURY SOURCES, edited by Jim Harter. 391 copyright-free wood engravings for artists and designers selected from rare periodicals. Most extensive such collection available. All illustrations in line. 128pp. 9 x 12. 23703-6 Pa. $4.50

ARABIC ART IN COLOR, Prisse d'Avennes. From the greatest ornamentalists of all time—50 plates in color, rarely seen outside the Near East, rich in suggestion and stimulus. Includes 4 plates on covers. 46pp. 9⅜ x 12¼. 23658-7 Pa. $6.00

AUTHENTIC ALGERIAN CARPET DESIGNS AND MOTIFS, edited by June Beveridge. Algerian carpets are world famous. Dozens of geometrical motifs are charted on grids, color-coded, for weavers, needleworkers, craftsmen, designers. 53 illustrations plus 4 in color. 48pp. 8¼ x 11. (Available in U.S. only) 23650-1 Pa. $1.75

DICTIONARY OF AMERICAN PORTRAITS, edited by Hayward and Blanche Cirker. 4000 important Americans, earliest times to 1905, mostly in clear line. Politicians, writers, soldiers, scientists, inventors, industrialists, Indians, Blacks, women, outlaws, etc. Identificatory information. 756pp. 9¼ x 12¾. 21823-6 Clothbd. $40.00

HOW THE OTHER HALF LIVES, Jacob A. Riis. Journalistic record of filth, degradation, upward drive in New York immigrant slums, shops, around 1900. New edition includes 100 original Riis photos, monuments of early photography. 233pp. 10 x 7⅞. 22012-5 Pa. $7.00

NEW YORK IN THE THIRTIES, Berenice Abbott. Noted photographer's fascinating study of city shows new buildings that have become famous and old sights that have disappeared forever. Insightful commentary. 97 photographs. 97pp. 11⅜ x 10. 22967-X Pa. $5.00

MEN AT WORK, Lewis W. Hine. Famous photographic studies of construction workers, railroad men, factory workers and coal miners. New supplement of 18 photos on Empire State building construction. New introduction by Jonathan L. Doherty. Total of 69 photos. 63pp. 8 x 10¾. 23475-4 Pa. $3.00

THE DEPRESSION YEARS AS PHOTOGRAPHED BY ARTHUR ROTH-STEIN, Arthur Rothstein. First collection devoted entirely to the work of outstanding 1930s photographer: famous dust storm photo, ragged children, unemployed, etc. 120 photographs. Captions. 119pp. 9¼ x 10¾.
23590-4 Pa. $5.00

CAMERA WORK: A PICTORIAL GUIDE, Alfred Stieglitz. All 559 illustrations and plates from the most important periodical in the history of art photography, *Camera Work* (1903-17). Presented four to a page, reduced in size but still clear, in strict chronological order, with complete captions. Three indexes. Glossary. Bibliography. 176pp. 8⅜ x 11¼.
23591-2 Pa. $6.95

ALVIN LANGDON COBURN, PHOTOGRAPHER, Alvin L. Coburn. Revealing autobiography by one of greatest photographers of 20th century gives insider's version of Photo-Secession, plus comments on his own work. 77 photographs by Coburn. Edited by Helmut and Alison Gernsheim. 160pp. 8⅛ x 11.
23685-4 Pa. $6.00

NEW YORK IN THE FORTIES, Andreas Feininger. 162 brilliant photographs by the well-known photographer, formerly with *Life* magazine, show commuters, shoppers, Times Square at night, Harlem nightclub, Lower East Side, etc. Introduction and full captions by John von Hartz. 181pp. 9¼ x 10¾.
23585-8 Pa. $6.95

GREAT NEWS PHOTOS AND THE STORIES BEHIND THEM, John Faber. Dramatic volume of 140 great news photos, 1855 through 1976, and revealing stories behind them, with both historical and technical information. Hindenburg disaster, shooting of Oswald, nomination of Jimmy Carter, etc. 160pp. 8¼ x 11.
23667-6 Pa. $5.00

THE ART OF THE CINEMATOGRAPHER, Leonard Maltin. Survey of American cinematography history and anecdotal interviews with 5 masters—Arthur Miller, Hal Mohr, Hal Rosson, Lucien Ballard, and Conrad Hall. Very large selection of behind-the-scenes production photos. 105 photographs. Filmographies. Index. Originally *Behind the Camera*. 144pp. 8¼ x 11.
23686-2 Pa. $5.00

DESIGNS FOR THE THREE-CORNERED HAT (LE TRICORNE), Pablo Picasso. 32 fabulously rare drawings—including 31 color illustrations of costumes and accessories—for 1919 production of famous ballet. Edited by Parmenia Migel, who has written new introduction. 48pp. 9⅜ x 12¼. (Available in U.S. only)
23709-5 Pa. $5.00

NOTES OF A FILM DIRECTOR, Sergei Eisenstein. Greatest Russian filmmaker explains montage, making of *Alexander Nevsky*, aesthetics; comments on self, associates, great rivals (Chaplin), similar material. 78 illustrations. 240pp. 5⅜ x 8½.
22392-2 Pa. $4.50

HOLLYWOOD GLAMOUR PORTRAITS, edited by John Kobal. 145 photos capture the stars from 1926-49, the high point in portrait photography. Gable, Harlow, Bogart, Bacall, Hedy Lamarr, Marlene Dietrich, Robert Montgomery, Marlon Brando, Veronica Lake; 94 stars in all. Full background on photographers, technical aspects, much more. Total of 160pp. 8⅜ x 11¼. 23352-9 Pa. $6.00

THE NEW YORK STAGE: FAMOUS PRODUCTIONS IN PHOTOGRAPHS, edited by Stanley Appelbaum. 148 photographs from Museum of City of New York show 142 plays, 1883-1939. *Peter Pan, The Front Page, Dead End, Our Town,* O'Neill, hundreds of actors and actresses, etc. Full indexes. 154pp. 9½ x 10. 23241-7 Pa. $6.00

DIALOGUES CONCERNING TWO NEW SCIENCES, Galileo Galilei. Encompassing 30 years of experiment and thought, these dialogues deal with geometric demonstrations of fracture of solid bodies, cohesion, leverage, speed of light and sound, pendulums, falling bodies, accelerated motion, etc. 300pp. 5⅜ x 8½. 60099-8 Pa. $4.00

THE GREAT OPERA STARS IN HISTORIC PHOTOGRAPHS, edited by James Camner. 343 portraits from the 1850s to the 1940s: Tamburini, Mario, Caliapin, Jeritza, Melchior, Melba, Patti, Pinza, Schipa, Caruso, Farrar, Steber, Gobbi, and many more—270 performers in all. Index. 199pp. 8⅜ x 11¼. 23575-0 Pa. $7.50

J. S. BACH, Albert Schweitzer. Great full-length study of Bach, life, background to music, music, by foremost modern scholar. Ernest Newman translation. 650 musical examples. Total of 928pp. 5⅜ x 8½. (Available in U.S. only) 21631-4, 21632-2 Pa., Two-vol. set $11.00

COMPLETE PIANO SONATAS, Ludwig van Beethoven. All sonatas in the fine Schenker edition, with fingering, analytical material. One of best modern editions. Total of 615pp. 9 x 12. (Available in U.S. only) 23134-8, 23135-6 Pa., Two-vol. set $15.50

KEYBOARD MUSIC, J. S. Bach. Bach-Gesellschaft edition. For harpsichord, piano, other keyboard instruments. English Suites, French Suites, Six Partitas, Goldberg Variations, Two-Part Inventions, Three-Part Sinfonias. 312pp. 8⅛ x 11. (Available in U.S. only) 22360-4 Pa. $6.95

FOUR SYMPHONIES IN FULL SCORE, Franz Schubert. Schubert's four most popular symphonies: No. 4 in C Minor ("Tragic"); No. 5 in B-flat Major; No. 8 in B Minor ("Unfinished"); No. 9 in C Major ("Great"). Breitkopf & Hartel edition. Study score. 261pp. 9⅜ x 12¼. 23681-1 Pa. $6.50

THE AUTHENTIC GILBERT & SULLIVAN SONGBOOK, W. S. Gilbert, A. S. Sullivan. Largest selection available; 92 songs, uncut, original keys, in piano rendering approved by Sullivan. Favorites and lesser-known fine numbers. Edited with plot synopses by James Spero. 3 illustrations. 399pp. 9 x 12. 23482-7 Pa. $9.95

PRINCIPLES OF ORCHESTRATION, Nikolay Rimsky-Korsakov. Great classical orchestrator provides fundamentals of tonal resonance, progression of parts, voice and orchestra, tutti effects, much else in major document. 330pp. of musical excerpts. 489pp. 6½ x 9¼.   21266-1 Pa. $7.50

TRISTAN UND ISOLDE, Richard Wagner. Full orchestral score with complete instrumentation. Do not confuse with piano reduction. Commentary by Felix Mottl, great Wagnerian conductor and scholar. Study score. 655pp. 8⅛ x 11.   22915-7 Pa. $13.95

REQUIEM IN FULL SCORE, Giuseppe Verdi. Immensely popular with choral groups and music lovers. Republication of edition published by C. F. Peters, Leipzig, n. d. German frontmaker in English translation. Glossary. Text in Latin. Study score. 204pp. 9⅜ x 12¼.
                    23682-X Pa. $6.00

COMPLETE CHAMBER MUSIC FOR STRINGS, Felix Mendelssohn. All of Mendelssohn's chamber music: Octet, 2 Quintets, 6 Quartets, and Four Pieces for String Quartet. (Nothing with piano is included). Complete works edition (1874-7). Study score. 283 pp. 9⅜ x 12¼.
                    23679-X Pa. $7.50

POPULAR SONGS OF NINETEENTH-CENTURY AMERICA, edited by Richard Jackson. 64 most important songs: "Old Oaken Bucket," "Arkansas Traveler," "Yellow Rose of Texas," etc. Authentic original sheet music, full introduction and commentaries. 290pp. 9 x 12.   23270-0 Pa. $7.95

COLLECTED PIANO WORKS, Scott Joplin. Edited by Vera Brodsky Lawrence. Practically all of Joplin's piano works—rags, two-steps, marches, waltzes, etc., 51 works in all. Extensive introduction by Rudi Blesh. Total of 345pp. 9 x 12.   23106-2 Pa. $14.95

BASIC PRINCIPLES OF CLASSICAL BALLET, Agrippina Vaganova. Great Russian theoretician, teacher explains methods for teaching classical ballet; incorporates best from French, Italian, Russian schools. 118 illustrations. 175pp. 5⅜ x 8½.   22036-2 Pa. $2.50

CHINESE CHARACTERS, L. Wieger. Rich analysis of 2300 characters according to traditional systems into primitives. Historical-semantic analysis to phonetics (Classical Mandarin) and radicals. 820pp. 6⅛ x 9¼.
                    21321-8 Pa. $10.00

EGYPTIAN LANGUAGE: EASY LESSONS IN EGYPTIAN HIERO-GLYPHICS, E. A. Wallis Budge. Foremost Egyptologist offers Egyptian grammar, explanation of hieroglyphics, many reading texts, dictionary of symbols. 246pp. 5 x 7½. (Available in U.S. only)
                    21394-3 Clothbd. $7.50

AN ETYMOLOGICAL DICTIONARY OF MODERN ENGLISH, Ernest Weekley. Richest, fullest work, by foremost British lexicographer. Detailed word histories. Inexhaustible. Do not confuse this with *Concise Etymological Dictionary*, which is abridged. Total of 856pp. 6½ x 9¼.
                    21873-2, 21874-0 Pa., Two-vol. set $12.00

A MAYA GRAMMAR, Alfred M. Tozzer. Practical, useful English-language grammar by the Harvard anthropologist who was one of the three greatest American scholars in the area of Maya culture. Phonetics, grammatical processes, syntax, more. 301pp. 5⅜ x 8½.   23465-7 Pa. $4.00

THE JOURNAL OF HENRY D. THOREAU, edited by Bradford Torrey, F. H. Allen. Complete reprinting of 14 volumes, 1837-61, over two million words; the sourcebooks for *Walden*, etc. Definitive. All original sketches, plus 75 photographs. Introduction by Walter Harding. Total of 1804pp. 8½ x 12¼.   20312-3, 20313-1 Clothbd., Two-vol. set $70.00

CLASSIC GHOST STORIES, Charles Dickens and others. 18 wonderful stories you've wanted to reread: "The Monkey's Paw," "The House and the Brain," "The Upper Berth," "The Signalman," "Dracula's Guest," "The Tapestried Chamber," etc. Dickens, Scott, Mary Shelley, Stoker, etc. 330pp. 5⅜ x 8½.   20735-8 Pa. $4.50

SEVEN SCIENCE FICTION NOVELS, H. G. Wells. Full novels. *First Men in the Moon, Island of Dr. Moreau, War of the Worlds, Food of the Gods, Invisible Man, Time Machine, In the Days of the Comet.* A basic science-fiction library. 1015pp. 5⅜ x 8½. (Available in U.S. only)
20264-X Clothbd. $8.95

ARMADALE, Wilkie Collins. Third great mystery novel by the author of *The Woman in White* and *The Moonstone.* Ingeniously plotted narrative shows an exceptional command of character, incident and mood. Original magazine version with 40 illustrations. 597pp. 5⅜ x 8½.
23429-0 Pa. $6.00

MASTERS OF MYSTERY, H. Douglas Thomson. The first book in English (1931) devoted to history and aesthetics of detective story. Poe, Doyle, LeFanu, Dickens, many others, up to 1930. New introduction and notes by E. F. Bleiler. 288pp. 5⅜ x 8½. (Available in U.S. only)
23606-4 Pa. $4.00

FLATLAND, E. A. Abbott. Science-fiction classic explores life of 2-D being in 3-D world. Read also as introduction to thought about hyperspace. Introduction by Banesh Hoffmann. 16 illustrations. 103pp. 5⅜ x 8½.
20001-9 Pa. $2.00

THREE SUPERNATURAL NOVELS OF THE VICTORIAN PERIOD, edited, with an introduction, by E. F. Bleiler. Reprinted complete and unabridged, three great classics of the supernatural: *The Haunted Hotel* by Wilkie Collins, *The Haunted House at Latchford* by Mrs. J. H. Riddell, and *The Lost Stradivarious* by J. Meade Falkner. 325pp. 5⅜ x 8½.
22571-2 Pa. $4.00

AYESHA: THE RETURN OF "SHE," H. Rider Haggard. Virtuoso sequel featuring the great mythic creation, Ayesha, in an adventure that is fully as good as the first book, *She.* Original magazine version, with 47 original illustrations by Maurice Greiffenhagen. 189pp. 6½ x 9¼.
23649-8 Pa. $3.50

UNCLE SILAS, J. Sheridan LeFanu. Victorian Gothic mystery novel, considered by many best of period, even better than Collins or Dickens. Wonderful psychological terror. Introduction by Frederick Shroyer. 436pp. 5⅜ x 8½.   21715-9 Pa. $6.00

JURGEN, James Branch Cabell. The great erotic fantasy of the 1920's that delighted thousands, shocked thousands more. Full final text, Lane edition with 13 plates by Frank Pape. 346pp. 5⅜ x 8½.
23507-6 Pa. $4.50

THE CLAVERINGS, Anthony Trollope. Major novel, chronicling aspects of British Victorian society, personalities. Reprint of Cornhill serialization, 16 plates by M. Edwards; first reprint of full text. Introduction by Norman Donaldson. 412pp. 5⅜ x 8½.   23464-9 Pa. $5.00

KEPT IN THE DARK, Anthony Trollope. Unusual short novel about Victorian morality and abnormal psychology by the great English author. Probably the first American publication. Frontispiece by Sir John Millais. 92pp. 6½ x 9¼.   23609-9 Pa. $2.50

RALPH THE HEIR, Anthony Trollope. Forgotten tale of illegitimacy, inheritance. Master novel of Trollope's later years. Victorian country estates, clubs, Parliament, fox hunting, world of fully realized characters. Reprint of 1871 edition. 12 illustrations by F. A. Faser. 434pp. of text. 5⅜ x 8½.   23642-0 Pa. $5.00

YEKL and THE IMPORTED BRIDEGROOM AND OTHER STORIES OF THE NEW YORK GHETTO, Abraham Cahan. Film *Hester Street* based on *Yekl* (1896). Novel, other stories among first about Jewish immigrants of N.Y.'s East Side. Highly praised by W. D. Howells—Cahan "a new star of realism." New introduction by Bernard G. Richards. 240pp. 5⅜ x 8½.   22427-9 Pa. $3.50

THE HIGH PLACE, James Branch Cabell. Great fantasy writer's enchanting comedy of disenchantment set in 18th-century France. Considered by some critics to be even better than his famous *Jurgen*. 10 illustrations and numerous vignettes by noted fantasy artist Frank C. Pape. 320pp. 5⅜ x 8½.   23670-6 Pa. $4.00

ALICE'S ADVENTURES UNDER GROUND, Lewis Carroll. Facsimile of ms. Carroll gave Alice Liddell in 1864. Different in many ways from final Alice. Handlettered, illustrated by Carroll. Introduction by Martin Gardner. 128pp. 5⅜ x 8½.   21482-6 Pa. $2.50

FAVORITE ANDREW LANG FAIRY TALE BOOKS IN MANY COLORS, Andrew Lang. The four Lang favorites in a boxed set—the complete *Red, Green, Yellow* and *Blue* Fairy Books. 164 stories; 439 illustrations by Lancelot Speed, Henry Ford and G. P. Jacomb Hood. Total of about 1500pp. 5⅜ x 8½.   23407-X Boxed set, Pa. $15.95

HOUSEHOLD STORIES BY THE BROTHERS GRIMM. All the great Grimm stories: "Rumpelstiltskin," "Snow White," "Hansel and Gretel," etc., with 114 illustrations by Walter Crane. 269pp. 5⅜ x 8½.
21080-4 Pa. $3.50

SLEEPING BEAUTY, illustrated by Arthur Rackham. Perhaps the fullest, most delightful version ever, told by C. S. Evans. Rackham's best work. 49 illustrations. 110pp. 7⅞ x 10¾. 22756-1 Pa. $2.50

AMERICAN FAIRY TALES, L. Frank Baum. Young cowboy lassoes Father Time; dummy in Mr. Floman's department store window comes to life; and 10 other fairy tales. 41 illustrations by N. P. Hall, Harry Kennedy, Ike Morgan, and Ralph Gardner. 209pp. 5⅜ x 8½. 23643-9 Pa. $3.00

THE WONDERFUL WIZARD OF OZ, L. Frank Baum. Facsimile in full color of America's finest children's classic. Introduction by Martin Gardner. 143 illustrations by W. W. Denslow. 267pp. 5⅜ x 8½.
20691-2 Pa. $3.50

THE TALE OF PETER RABBIT, Beatrix Potter. The inimitable Peter's terrifying adventure in Mr. McGregor's garden, with all 27 wonderful, full-color Potter illustrations. 55pp. 4¼ x 5½. (Available in U.S. only)
22827-4 Pa. $1.25

THE STORY OF KING ARTHUR AND HIS KNIGHTS, Howard Pyle. Finest children's version of life of King Arthur. 48 illustrations by Pyle. 131pp. 6⅛ x 9¼. 21445-1 Pa. $4.95

CARUSO'S CARICATURES, Enrico Caruso. Great tenor's remarkable caricatures of self, fellow musicians, composers, others. Toscanini, Puccini, Farrar, etc. Impish, cutting, insightful. 473 illustrations. Preface by M. Sisca. 217pp. 8⅜ x 11¼. 23528-9 Pa. $6.95

PERSONAL NARRATIVE OF A PILGRIMAGE TO ALMADINAH AND MECCAH, Richard Burton. Great travel classic by remarkably colorful personality. Burton, disguised as a Moroccan, visited sacred shrines of Islam, narrowly escaping death. Wonderful observations of Islamic life, customs, personalities. 47 illustrations. Total of 959pp. 5⅜ x 8½.
21217-3, 21218-1 Pa., Two-vol. set $12.00

INCIDENTS OF TRAVEL IN YUCATAN, John L. Stephens. Classic (1843) exploration of jungles of Yucatan, looking for evidences of Maya civilization. Travel adventures, Mexican and Indian culture, etc. Total of 669pp. 5⅜ x 8½. 20926-1, 20927-X Pa., Two-vol. set $7.90

AMERICAN LITERARY AUTOGRAPHS FROM WASHINGTON IRVING TO HENRY JAMES, Herbert Cahoon, et al. Letters, poems, manuscripts of Hawthorne, Thoreau, Twain, Alcott, Whitman, 67 other prominent American authors. Reproductions, full transcripts and commentary. Plus checklist of all American Literary Autographs in The Pierpont Morgan Library. Printed on exceptionally high-quality paper. 136 illustrations. 212pp. 9⅛ x 12¼. 23548-3 Pa. $12.50

AN AUTOBIOGRAPHY, Margaret Sanger. Exciting personal account of hard-fought battle for woman's right to birth control, against prejudice, church, law. Foremost feminist document. 504pp. 5⅜ x 8½.
20470-7 Pa. $5.50

MY BONDAGE AND MY FREEDOM, Frederick Douglass. Born as a slave, Douglass became outspoken force in antislavery movement. The best of Douglass's autobiographies. Graphic description of slave life. Introduction by P. Foner. 464pp. 5⅜ x 8½.
22457-0 Pa. $5.50

LIVING MY LIFE, Emma Goldman. Candid, no holds barred account by foremost American anarchist: her own life, anarchist movement, famous contemporaries, ideas and their impact. Struggles and confrontations in America, plus deportation to U.S.S.R. Shocking inside account of persecution of anarchists under Lenin. 13 plates. Total of 944pp. 5⅜ x 8½.
22543-7, 22544-5 Pa., Two-vol. set $12.00

LETTERS AND NOTES ON THE MANNERS, CUSTOMS AND CONDITIONS OF THE NORTH AMERICAN INDIANS, George Catlin. Classic account of life among Plains Indians: ceremonies, hunt, warfare, etc. Dover edition reproduces for first time all original paintings. 312 plates. 572pp. of text. 6⅛ x 9¼.
22118-0, 22119-9 Pa.. Two-vol. set $12.00

THE MAYA AND THEIR NEIGHBORS, edited by Clarence L. Hay, others. Synoptic view of Maya civilization in broadest sense, together with Northern, Southern neighbors. Integrates much background, valuable detail not elsewhere. Prepared by greatest scholars: Kroeber, Morley, Thompson, Spinden, Vaillant, many others. Sometimes called Tozzer Memorial Volume. 60 illustrations, linguistic map. 634pp. 5⅜ x 8½.
23510-6 Pa. $10.00

HANDBOOK OF THE INDIANS OF CALIFORNIA, A. L. Kroeber. Foremost American anthropologist offers complete ethnographic study of each group. Monumental classic. 459 illustrations, maps. 995pp. 5⅜ x 8½.
23368-5 Pa. $13.00

SHAKTI AND SHAKTA, Arthur Avalon. First book to give clear, cohesive analysis of Shakta doctrine, Shakta ritual and Kundalini Shakti (yoga). Important work by one of world's foremost students of Shaktic and Tantric thought. 732pp. 5⅜ x 8½. (Available in U.S. only)
23645-5 Pa. $7.95

AN INTRODUCTION TO THE STUDY OF THE MAYA HIEROGLYPHS, Syvanus Griswold Morley. Classic study by one of the truly great figures in hieroglyph research. Still the best introduction for the student for reading Maya hieroglyphs. New introduction by J. Eric S. Thompson. 117 illustrations. 284pp. 5⅜ x 8½.
23108-9 Pa. $4.00

A STUDY OF MAYA ART, Herbert J. Spinden. Landmark classic interprets Maya symbolism, estimates styles, covers ceramics, architecture, murals, stone carvings as artforms. Still a basic book in area. New introduction by J. Eric Thompson. Over 750 illustrations. 341pp. 8⅜ x 11¼.
21235-1 Pa. $6.95

GEOMETRY, RELATIVITY AND THE FOURTH DIMENSION, Rudolf Rucker. Exposition of fourth dimension, means of visualization, concepts of relativity as Flatland characters continue adventures. Popular, easily followed yet accurate, profound. 141 illustrations. 133pp. 5⅜ x 8½.
23400-2 Pa. $2.75

THE ORIGIN OF LIFE, A. I. Oparin. Modern classic in biochemistry, the first rigorous examination of possible evolution of life from nitrocarbon compounds. Non-technical, easily followed. Total of 295pp. 5⅜ x 8½.
60213-3 Pa. $4.00

PLANETS, STARS AND GALAXIES, A. E. Fanning. Comprehensive introductory survey: the sun, solar system, stars, galaxies, universe, cosmology; quasars, radio stars, etc. 24pp. of photographs. 189pp. 5⅜ x 8½. (Available in U.S. only)
21680-2 Pa. $3.75

THE THIRTEEN BOOKS OF EUCLID'S ELEMENTS, translated with introduction and commentary by Sir Thomas L. Heath. Definitive edition. Textual and linguistic notes, mathematical analysis, 2500 years of critical commentary. Do not confuse with abridged school editions. Total of 1414pp. 5⅜ x 8½.
60088-2, 60089-0, 60090-4 Pa., Three-vol. set $18.50

Prices subject to change without notice.

Available at your book dealer or write for free catalogue to Dept. GI, Dover Publications, Inc., 180 Varick St., N.Y., N.Y. 10014. Dover publishes more than 175 books each year on science, elementary and advanced mathematics, biology, music, art, literary history, social sciences and other areas.